THE NEW TESTAMENT
APOCRYPHA

IS VOLUME

72

OF THE

Twentieth Century Encyclopedia of Catholicism

UNDER SECTION

VI

THE WORD OF GOD

IT IS ALSO THE

53RD

VOLUME IN ORDER OF PUBLICATION

Edited by HENRI DANIEL-ROPS of the Académie Française

THE NEW TESTAMENT APOCRYPHA

By *JACQUES HERVIEUX*

Translated from the French by DOM WULSTAN HIBBERD

HAWTHORN BOOKS · PUBLISHERS · *New York*

First Edition, November, 1960

NIHIL OBSTAT

Rt. Rev. Msgr. Joseph H. Brady, S.T.D.

Censor Librorum

IMPRIMATUR

Most Reverend Thomas A. Boland, S.T.D.

Archbishop of Newark

Newark, November 28, 1960

CONTENTS

INTRODUCTION

WHAT THE GOSPEL DOES NOT TELL US

We think we know the Gospel story, because we have been familiar with its characters and scenes since childhood. Has not familiarity blunted our real knowledge? A little attention from a fresh angle will quickly give rise to a thousand and one questions on the subject. In fact, the early Christians have already asked these questions, with an acuteness that is difficult to believe today. The Gospel has not told us everything about Jesus, his Mother or the apostles. There was an eagerness to know more about their person, life and message. These questions arose owing to the silence and great reserve of the Bible: this child, called Mary, whom God wished to be the Virgin Mother of his Son, how was she born, and what was her childhood like? How had Providence disposed the virginal birth of the Messiah? Did our Lady, when she finished her course, know the death that is common to us mortals? And did not the Infant Jesus from his earliest age, reveal his Divinity to the world through his knowledge and miracles? In addition to what the evangelists have left us, has not perhaps some secret revelation preserved various unwritten words of the Master? And what had happened to the ever-Living Lord during his passage through death? How did his resurrection actually happen? Then, when had the apostles gone to preach? What sort of death had ended their missionary labours? How do the saved and the damned fare in the next world?

It may be thought that some of these questions arise from idle curiosity. Many of them are, indeed, born of that vivid imagination of the populace from which early Christianity drew its adherents. But we can share some of the ardent zeal of these first Christians. They loved to meditate on the striking events which accompanied the birth of the Messiah, his saving mission and the ever new history of the Church he founded. Priceless memories of eye-witnesses about Jesus and the early disciples were lovingly passed from mouth to mouth. It was still the Word of the Master which these voices re-echoed.

While the selection of deeds and words of our Saviour collected in the Gospel was devoutedly read, oral traditions, at first more or less verifiable, continued to circulate at large. These soon crystallized in writings, which afforded an answer to inquiring minds.

THE APOCRYPHAL WRITINGS

These writings which arose from within the Christian communities between the first and the sixth centuries, have this in common: they adopted the same form in which just a little earlier the Good News had been moulded. Thus, we can read gospels especially, but also acts of the apostles, epistles and apocalypses, similar to those of the New Testament.

To this varied and plentiful literature, which emerged very rapidly on the lines of the sacred books, we give the name of the apocryphal writings. This word comes from the Greek ἀπόκρυφα which means "hidden things." It would appear, then, that at first it meant secret books in which certain sects preserved their revelations for their own associates. And we see how the Church from the very first, forbade as false Scriptures, these strange and mystical speculations, as incompatible with the sacred and perfectly clear teaching of Christ.

But the title apocryphal has not been reserved for those

books only which the Church condemned for false doctrine. The name was extended to cover all writings which
were not recognized as inspired writings, and which for
that reason were not included in the list of the sacred
Scriptures. Under this heading were found works whose
doctrine was true and sound, and which the Fathers allowed to be used privately, but forbade to be read publicly at the meetings of Christians.

Enough has been said to show the interest that will be
found in the list of this great library—today too often
forgotten—wherein the early times of Christianity live
again. Side by side with books greatly suspect, we shall
find excellent works, the heirs of authentic traditions, but
in which the primitive truths have been deformed or fool-
ishly amplified by popular imagination. Some of them are
a noble apologetic for and a reflection of the faith of all
the early centuries. Though the Church, ever careful of
guarding the purity of the Gospel message unsullied, has
not accepted them as the Word of God—for so many
fables and idle tales have gained currency under the title
of gospel—she does not deny that these are an expression,
and often a right and profound one, of her tradition.

The apocryphal writings set out to tell us what the
Gospels do not say. But the reader cannot realize too
strongly that a whole world of beauty, truth and depth
separates the Gospel from its imitations. One thing is certain; the apocryphal writings have added nothing to Revelation. Their doctrinal rôle has been entirely secondary:
dogma is not based on them, but on a growing understanding, at once wise and prudent, of Scripture. Yet we
do find intuitions of the Faith in the apocryphal writings,
since they have been produced by the Christian mind. It
would be ungracious to forget that many of these writings
represent reflection on Scripture, upon which the Fathers
nourished their thought, and are a witness to the origins

of Catholic theology. Nor must we overlook their influence on Christian literature and art—especially in the Middle Ages—an influence which has contributed not a little to inform the mind and heart of the faithful. Nor should we ignore their use in the liturgy itself, for the apocryphal writings have powerfully aided the cultus of our Lady and the apostles.

In short, a whole collection of "traditions" or of ideas which are familiar to us today, have their unique source in the apocryphal writings. In them a new field is opened to our exploration, that of the history and life and thought of the primitive Church. In an age which desires above all a return to sources, this incursion into writings on the fringe of the inspired Scriptures will have a twofold advantage: to make us understand better by contrast the truth of the Gospel, and at the same time to appreciate more sympathetically this living voice of oral Tradition from which generations of the faithful have drawn.

A good edition of the principal apocryphal writings exists (See Select Bibliography at the end of this volume). Here our intention is to examine the best of these by contrasting them with their source and models, the inspired Gospels. It is not sufficient for the reader to study these curious documents of the early centuries; he needs a commentary to explain them step by step. From this may ensue profitable discussion leading to doctrinal clarification which will enable the twentieth-century Christian to be fully informed on all the points of his faith.

PART I

THE STORY OF MARY, VIRGIN AND MOTHER

CHAPTER I

THE OLDEST TRADITIONS
CONCERNING MARY

THE GOSPEL

The Virgin Mary is the most unobtrusive of all the characters of the Gospel, a paradox which has always astonished the thoughtful reader of the life of Jesus. In those wonderful passages from which we can conclude that, after her son, she is the chief actor in the sacred drama, the Blessed Virgin, however, appears but little. In the whole of the New Testament we can find scarcely a dozen allusions to her. This is not just accidental. If, at first sight, Mary appears to be only an accessory in the work of salvation, her presence and work are in truth profoundly important to it. It was through her that our Saviour came into the world. She, the Mother of God, while apparently in the background like all mothers, was yet deeply involved in the mission and destiny of her Child. When we understand what the mystery is of which Mary forms a part it is not difficult to appreciate the extreme reticence of the Scriptural narrative.

It should not be forgotten, also, that the evangelists did not set out to write a life of our Lady, relating all her actions. The task with which Christ had entrusted them was to announce the Good News of salvation. Their plan was limited to this: to narrate the main events through

which our Saviour had achieved his work: to witness publicly to his words and miracles, and especially to his death
and resurrection. The cataclysmic events of our salvation
are centred upon Christ, not upon Mary. She had her part
to play in them, and that was enough.

This explains why the sacred writers have not preserved
any of the day to day details of her earthly course. Scripture gives us no description of her birth and childhood,
nor of her adult life and death. Yet her maternal care and
her vital part in the divine mystery of salvation are not on
that account missing. In particular St Luke, but also St
Matthew have preserved, in passages of supreme beauty,
the precise instant of her calling, the moment when this
woman—blessed among all others—was called to become
the mother of the Messiah. St John in his turn has produced an outline sketch of her who, in Jesus' footsteps till
Calvary itself, merited to become the Mother of all believers. Lastly, a passage in the Acts of the Apostles
(1.14) shows that Mary was present at the birth of the
Church.

Just a few passing references, here and there, very slight
in all. But the believer, on closing the Gospel, has found
in them the authentic portrait of Mary.

TRADITION

Everything else is of little consequence. A certain passage of time has been necessary—twenty centuries of reflection on the Gospel were required for the Church to
have a more revealing picture of this greatly privileged
being. That unceasing line of thought known as oral tradition, which the community of believers owes to the original events, has emphasized certain features in Mary's portrait. Yet it must be admitted that a choice has been made
among the great quantity of writings on Mary which have

come down to us. For the Church, the guardian of the Gospel and of the truths contained in it, cannot permit any additions to the deposit of faith. She has only allowed the most careful scrutiny to be made.

The following pages offer an account of these ancient traditions about our Lady and a critical examination of them.

THE GOSPEL OF PSEUDO-JAMES

The first Christian communities jealously preserved certain memories of Jesus' Mother. It was perfectly natural for them eagerly to desire a life of Mary containing additional information about the most important, though the most unobtrusive, person in the Gospels, after Jesus himself. Faith provoked more than one question requiring an answer. Who were the privileged folk destined by God to bring Mary into the world? How had this little girl grown up before God and among her fellow beings that she should have merited the title of Virgin? What divine plan had led to her encountering Joseph? And lastly, how had she given birth to the Messiah without losing her virginity? The apostles and their immediate disciples had left no written information on these matters. Perhaps at least some of the coveted information was obtained from them orally.

From the beginning of the second century—less than a century after Mary's death—stories began to circulate which claimed to have originated from apostolic circles. While it is difficult to distinguish historical details from the legends which soon became mixed up with them, a corpus of oral tradition soon took shape in the form, then popular and widespread, of a "gospel."

This "gospel" was attributed to the Apostle James. In the early Greek manuscripts in which it was written, the work did not always boast the title of gospel, but was more modestly called "The narrative of James on the birth of the holy Mother of God."

But this narrative did not only deal with our Lady's birth, but also and especially with her adolescence and marriage with Joseph and the birth of Jesus. In short, in less than twenty-five chapters, it was a real "Life of our Lady."

But the gospel presentation of this narrative did not deceive William Postel, the French scholar of the sixteenth century, who translated it into Latin with the subtitle of *the protevangelium of James*. The word *protevangelium* means "book which precedes the Gospel." This scholar explains that the title well fitted this work of James, which was a kind of preface to the Gospel of St Luke, who opens his "good news" with the story of the incidents immediately connected with Jesus' birth.[1] And this is exactly the case: James' story of our Lady sets out to tell the story of the events which had long prepared the Messiah's coming.

As we now have it, the work would seem to date from A.D. 130-140 and so is fairly near the events narrated. But no scholar today believes that the real author was St James the Less, first bishop of Jerusalem. As we know, it was the custom among the Jews to ascribe an anonymous work to the pen of some important person of the past. This method of "pseudonymity" was used to give importance to a work by borrowing a false name which endowed it with authority. The author of *pseudo-James* was anxious to protect his work with the apostolic authority of a contemporary of Mary.

We shall return later to the question of the historical value of this work. For the moment we can say that it

[1] Chapters 1 and 2 of St Luke form what is called the "Gospel of the Infancy" of Christ.

enjoyed at the outset a distinct success and was assured of not sinking into oblivion. Written, quite certainly, by a Jewish Christian, it quickly circulated from the East to the West. It gained prestige both from its real literary beauty and the perfect orthodoxy of its thought. But when it passed into the western world it necessarily changed its language. And, in being translated from Greek into Latin, it underwent certain retouches and transformations and really became another work.

THE GOSPEL OF PSEUDO-MATTHEW

About the sixth century there appeared in Latin a certain *book on the birth of the Blessed Mary and of the Saviour's infancy*. An introductory letter presented this new work as a "supplement" to the Gospel of St Matthew, translated personally by St Jerome the great fourth-century exegete.[2] What are we to make of this claim? We know that St Jerome, besides his Latin translation of the whole Bible, turned his attention to several of the apocryphal gospels current in his time. Perhaps he did believe that one of these was an original of the Gospel according to St Matthew.[3] But was it the book mentioned here? The numerous works of Jerome and his undoubted quality as an interpreter of the Bible have caused many spurious works to be fathered on to him. For—and this is an indication that it is spurious—how is it likely that the Apostle Matthew who was so restrained in his account of the infancy of Christ, would have added much later a long supplement of twenty chapters?

We have only to look at this so-called "supplement" to St Matthew's Gospel to be convinced that it is nothing more than a clever rearrangement of pseudo-James which

[2] An exegete is literally "one who interprets" the Scriptures.
[3] See below "the Gospel according to the Nazarenes," p. 141.

is thus entirely disguised. Throughout the narrative we find amplifications, embellishment and often deliberate corrections in incidents in the former work. An unknown author has changed the old Eastern traditions about the Blessed Virgin to suit the Latin West.

Compared with its source pseudo-Matthew brings out the differences of view which enable us to judge the evolution of popular belief about Mary between the second and fourth centuries. We shall use both traditions in so far as they complement each other. But before we go further we ought to discuss their historicity and doctrinal value.

History or Legend?

It is easy enough to understand the purposes behind these apocryphal gospels of James and Matthew. It was twofold: to fill in the gaps in the *curriculum vitae* of Mary's life in the canonical Gospels: secondly, to prove to readers a truth, merely stated in Scripture, that Mary is at the same time Virgin and Mother.

So we are dealing with works which set out to edify their readers in revealing Mary's virtues, and to prove to them, so far as this can be done, her virginal child-bearing.

Must we then ask whether we are dealing with history or legend? In reality, the nature of these works forbids our posing this question. For one reason, the ancients had no idea of purely objective history in the modern sense of the term. They did not simply relate the facts for their own sake: their "historical" literature was biassed, it was intended to support a thesis. Furthermore, the East, where the kind of narration we call "popular history" had its origins, readily mixed legends with the events related, so that it is impossible to separate from the historical nucleus what is purely imaginary.

It must be admitted that the gospels of pseudo-James and pseudo-Matthew belong to that form of literature which is neither strictly historical nor simply mythological. Specialists who speak of "historical romances" in the West, call this kind of writing in the East *Midrash Haggadah,* meaning a narrative which embroiders the biblical text for the purpose of edification.

Two elements make up this kind of writing: the *Haggadah* and the *Midrash.* We add a word on each.

An Edifying Narrative

The Haggadah is a "story" which contains some subject of religious edification. It has no other purpose than to teach, to bring out the moral or spiritual lesson founded on the facts. The Bible had already used this kind of writing. Books such as Job, Daniel, Tobias or Judith had made the great figures of their national past live once again to edify contemporary Israelites. The source of these devout stories was found in the treasury of popular oral traditions, and their assertions had no historical pretensions. The story of the Virgin Mary by James and Matthew is of this kind; it was not unlike "a life of a saint" such as was read at a later period in the Middle Ages, and its purpose principally was to exalt Mary's virginity. Although not strictly historical, the Haggadah, it must be remembered, has its roots in history. The oriental memory, if it puts the facts together somewhat quaintly, is not insensitive to the realities and depths of life. Where does history end and legend begin? We cannot answer this with any finality.

Based on Scripture

The Haggadah is supported and interpreted by the Midrash. This later word means a narrative which is based on the inspired writings to bring out what will be accomplished in due course. It is well known that the Jews, and then the early Christians, following their example, eagerly searched the Scriptures to find in them prophetic announcements of the events of our Salvation. This scouting[4] was wholly justified, because Christ was to fulfil all the former prophecies. The evangelists and writers of the New Testament have also given their meditation on the life of Jesus, in the light of the promises which he fulfilled. Passages of the Bible which they had hitherto found very obscure took on a new meaning in the light of what had happened; a divine prediction had come to pass. Already, the authors of the sapiential books of the Old Testament, understanding that God's plan would be achieved by stages, on the basis of the earlier sacred text had revealed the meaning of the events through which they lived.

The story of the Virgin Mary in pseudo-James and pseudo-Matthew is likewise based on the sacred writings to reveal even the slightest indications of the fulfilment of the divine will in the life of the Mother of Jesus. But the apocryphal writers have indulged too freely in this, of itself legitimate, reflection on the biblical data. Although in the divine plan the Virgin Mary accomplished her part in the work of salvation, so long foretold, did she fulfil to the letter the types assigned to her? Certainly not. Historical truth is measured by the gap between prophetic announcement and its fulfilment: the fulfilment always surpasses the idea that had been formed of it. As we shall see, whole episodes in the *Life of Mary* are nothing more than a literary reproduction of some Old Testament scene. Further, and this is the crowning error, both pseudo-James and his later imitation treat prophecy the wrong way round; unable to find foretold in the inspired text everything that they wish to see fulfilled in Mary they have manipulated it to make it agree with their ideas. Frequently, they base some new occurrence on a tiny and very obscure verse of the Bible. Imagination here outruns

[4] *Midrash* in Hebrew means "biblical investigation."

common sense and honesty in dealing with the Word of God.

The continual licence taken with the truth of Revelation creates an impenetrable gulf between the sacred Scriptures and these imitations sadly lacking in inspiration. The edifying stories we shall read, even when based on Scripture, are far from having the authority they claim; it was necessary to be fully aware of this before studying them and this was the purpose of our analysis of their literary form.

Doctrinal Interest

Although of no great historical value the apocryphal gospels of the Virgin Mary have a distinct value doctrinally; they inform us what were the beliefs of the early Christians about Mary. The gospel of James particularly is a popular expression of Christian belief about Mary at the beginning of the second century. Its very existence shows that from the first the Mother of Christ had already acquired such great repute that it was thought necessary to write a "Life of the Saint," the first of its kind.

There can be no doubt that the author answered a vital need. But it is important to emphasize that he was not content just to be a collector of traditions that were already old: he compiled a genuine treatise on the virginal Motherhood of Mary.

For it was in the second century that the attacks against Christ's virgin birth began. It looks as if the author composed this small treatise in an attempt to contend with them. All the narratives desire to maintain that the Mother of the Messiah was a virgin in her childbirth, so that the work could be called "A defence and explanation of the virginal Motherhood of Mary." That the book is not quite on a level with its aim does not detract from its interest. We have here valuable testimony—from the very fact of its antiquity—to Catholic belief in the virginity of Christ's Mother. It is easy to understand how all these ancient beliefs have been carefully collected by the Church who uses them in her liturgy. After the Gospel we have no earlier or more interesting witness to the divine rôle which the Blessed Virgin played in the economy of salvation. Doubtless these "gospels" are not inspired, but they are entitled to the respect due to primitive oral tradition. This justified the careful attention we shall give to them, at a time when the sources of Marian theology are the subject of investigation.

CHAPTER II

THE MIRACULOUS BIRTH

OF MARY

The canonical Gospels tell us absolutely nothing of Mary's infancy. She appears to be unknown to them until she is of marriageable age and is "espoused to Joseph" (Matt. 1. 18. Cf. Luke 1. 27). Who were her parents? How did she come into the world? How did she pass the time of her childhood? The apocryphal gospels obligingly endeavour to elucidate many of these points on which we remain in ignorance.

THE BARRENNESS OF JOACHIM AND ANNE

Neither Matthew nor Luke—the only two evangelists who tell us anything of Christ's infancy—have attempted to give us any information about our Saviour's maternal ancestors. The two genealogies which they have compiled deal not with Mary but with Joseph (Matt. 1. 16; Luke 3. 23).[1] So we do not even know the names of Mary's parents.

The Protevangelium of James has informed us of them. His narrative provides us with the family background of

[1] The reason for this is quite simple: by his legal paternity Joseph who was "of the house of David" conferred on Jesus all his hereditary rights, and consequently those of the Messianic line to which he belonged. This was more important than the maternal descent of his mother.

the Blessed Virgin. Thus we learn that her father was
called Joachim and her mother Anne. The author tells us
that he has learned the names and other facts about these
two persons "in the histories of the twelve tribes of Israel." Does he refer to some public register? It is hardly
likely for the Gospels would have known of them. We
should rather think of "histories" as traditions, either oral
or written, which were current about ancient Jewish fami-
lies. And this is what they tell us.

Joachim was a rich and devout man. And with his riches
"he made a double offering to the temple saying: What I
give of my superfluity shall be for all: I offer it in expiation
of my sins" (Prot. 1. 1). Could we find a man more generous towards God or his fellows. And yet Joachim was
not reputed a saint. He was held to be a "just" man; this
special term meant a man whose virtue was rewarded by
heaven with a numerous posterity and many divine bless-
ings. Now, although Joachim was devout he had no children, for his wife Anne was barren. Both were then
stumbling blocks to their neighbours who doubted their
virtue.

One day when Joachim, as was his custom, had come
to make a generous offering at the altar, he stood rebuked:
"It is not right for you to offer gifts first, for you have
begotten no offspring in Israel" (Prot. 1. 2). Joachim was
overcome with sadness and at the advice of his relations
consulted the tribal records of his people. He did indeed
find that all the just had raised up children in Israel. But
in his deep humiliation "he remembered the patriarch
Abraham, how God had given him a son in his last days,
Isaac" (Prot. 1. 3).

Leaving his wife, the devout Israelite went into the
desert with the idea of forcing God's hand by fasting and
prayer. His wife Anne wept bitterly at the departure of
her husband and at her barrenness. "I will bewail my

widowhood," she said, "and I will bewail my barrenness" (Prot. 1. 3).

There was certainly no greater misfortune for a Jew than to be childless, for had not God promised to his people a posterity like the sands of the sea? Every woman was deeply impressed with these promises, and if she were barren believed herself an object of God's displeasure. Anne poured forth her soul in bitter complaint: "Who begat me, and what womb brought me forth that I should be a reproach in Israel" (Prot. 3. 1).

Even her maidservant mocked her, and added to her bitterness. Anne remembered, however, the faith of her ancestors, and took heart to make this prayer: "God of my Fathers, bless me: hear my prayer, as you blessed the womb of Sara, and gave her a son, Isaac!" (Prot. 2. 4). And, against all hope, her prayer was heard: "Behold an angel of the Lord appeared to her and said: Anne, Anne, the Lord has heard your prayer: you shall conceive and bear, and your son shall be spoken of in the whole world" (Prot. 4. 1).

This wonderful message immediately found an echo in the soul of the afflicted Anne who believed at once in the angel's word. We can imagine that we hear our Lady's "fiat" already. And in an outpouring of faith she who was to be Mary's mother immediately consecrated her future offspring, making this vow: "As the Lord lives, if I bring forth either a male or female child, it shall minister to him all the days of its life" (Prot. 4. 1).

This vow was indeed a special pledge of the future. But it was now God's province to accomplish the angel's message.

JOACHIM AND ANNE ARE VINDICATED

Joachim and Anne had experienced public reproach in the time of their trial, for their worth before God was held in doubt. God now came to vindicate them in the eyes of everyone. While Anne was still overcome by the good news two other heavenly messengers told her that her husband would shortly return: "Behold your husband Joachim is coming with his flocks, for an angel of the Lord appeared to him saying: Joachim, Joachim, the Lord has heard your prayer. Go on your way, for your wife has conceived" (Prot. 4. 2). Divinely warned to leave his solitude, Joachim hurried to rejoin his wife.

A very understandable emotion filled husband and wife at their meeting. To their intimate sorrow had been added the pang of separation. So the joy which rose in Joachim's heart as he reached his home can be imagined. As for Anne, she only lived for the time of happiness in which she would be united again with her husband in a union no longer sterile.

With an extreme delicacy the Protevangelium of James recounts this tender reunion: "and behold Joachim came with his flocks, and Anne stood at the gate. When she saw him she ran and hung on his neck, saying to him: now I know that the Lord God has blessed me exceedingly, for I was as a widow, and I am so no longer: I was childless and I shall conceive. And Joachim rested the first day in his house" (Prot. 4. 4).

Later writers have described this scene as occurring not in the privacy of their house, but at the gates of Jerusalem, with a view to making this memorable reunion even more spectacular.[2] This is the famous meeting at the Golden

[2] In the East it is the custom for all public activities to take place at the gates of the town.

Gate which pseudo-Matthew has described in one of the most beautiful passages of the apocryphal literature:

> And when after thirty days occupied in going back, Joachim (and his shepherds and flocks) was near at hand, behold the angel of the Lord appeared to Anne, who was standing and praying, and said: go to the Gate which is called Golden, and meet thy husband in the way, for today he will come to thee. She therefore went to him in haste with her maidens, and praying to the Lord, she stood a long time in the gate waiting for him. And when she was wearied with the long wait, she raised her eyes and saw Joachim far off, coming with his flocks. And she ran to him and hung on his neck and gave thanks to God . . . and there was great joy among all their neighbours and acquaintances, so that the whole land of Israel congratulated them. (Ps-Matt. 3. 5).

Popular devotion, with the help of delightful works of art, was subsequently fond of dwelling on the story of this couple, whose good name was restored by God, joyfully embracing each other at the gateway of the Holy City. Heaven had indeed undertaken the justification of its holy ones. What Joachim had learnt from an angel in the course of a dream could now be disclosed to all: "The deeds of mercy which you and your wife Anne have done have been told in the presence of the Most High; and to you God will give such fruit as no prophet or saint has ever had from the beginning, or ever will have" (Ps-Matt. 3. 4). This solemn prophecy augured well of the event which was to come to pass in the home of this devout couple: the birth of the Virgin Mary.

MARY, THE CHILD OF MIRACLE

All happened as heaven had foretold: "And her months were fulfilled, and in the ninth month Anne conceived. And she asked the midwife: What have I brought forth?

And she said a girl. And Anne said: my soul is magnified this day, and she laid herself down. And when the days were fulfilled, Anne purified herself and gave suck to the child and called her name Mary" (Prot. 5. 2). Thus did the once barren Anne give birth miraculously to Mary.

There are parallels to this story in the miraculous births of certain figures in the biblical narrative. Whenever God had ordained someone to a particular mission, scripture emphasizes the supernatural nature of his birth. Frequently it surrounds their birth with a host of wonders. For instance Isaac, against all expectation, was the fruit of the old age of Abraham (Gen. 18. 10-15). It was not without reason that the author of the Protevangelium inspired in the hearts of Mary's parents the memory of the great patriarch and his barren wife. Both couples had no heir, but God remembered their faith, and in spite of their old age, gave them the promised child.

Even more similar to Mary are the births of Samuel and John the Baptist. The first was to be the head of a long line of prophets. His mother, who was also called Anne (Anna) had for a long time hoped for a child. Though they had no child, this woman and Elcana her husband were faithful in the fulfilment of their religious duties. But Anne's life was a martyrdom, for she endured the taunts of a rival who had had a child by her husband. One day being unable to bear up any longer she poured out her grief of soul before God in the Temple: "Sad at heart, she prayed to the Lord with many tears, and made a vow: Lord of hosts, if thou take heed of this sorrow I bear, if thou wilt keep this handmaid of thine ever in remembrance, and grant her a son, then he shall be my gift to the Lord all his life long" (I Kings 1. 10-11). God's heart was touched by the sorrow of this poor woman: "And the Lord bethought him of Anna, when next Elcana took her to his bed; so, in due time, she conceived and bore him a son. The name she gave him was Samuel" (I Kings 1. 20).

St Luke relates similar circumstances surrounding the birth of John the Baptist. The man who was to be the forerunner of Christ, and prepare for his immediate coming, was not born as the rest of men. His parents, Elizabeth and Zachary "were both well approved of God, following all the commandments and observances of the Lord without reproach. They had no child. Elizabeth was barren, and both were now well advanced in years" (Luke 1. 6-7).

While he was performing his priestly function in the Temple, for he was of the priestly order, Zachary was visited by an angel:

> Zachary, do not be afraid: thy prayer has been heard, and thy wife Elizabeth is to bear thee a son; to whom thou shalt give the name of John. . . . It was after these days that she conceived. . . . It is the Lord, she said who has done this thing for me, visiting me at his own time, to take away my reproach among men. [And the day came when] Elizabeth's time had come for her childbearing and she bore a son. Her neighbours and her kinsfolk, hearing how wonderfully God had showed his mercy to her, came to rejoice with her. (Luke 1. 13-58).

THE LESSON OF THE NARRATIVE

These literary comparisons are instructive. On each occasion an identical story is worked out with varying details: a profoundly religious husband and wife, leading exemplary lives, are unable to have a child. These parents are an object of ridicule to their neighbours but they lay their suffering before God, for whom nothing is impossible (Luke 1. 37). The prayer of the righteous is heard and the child who is born with the blessing of heaven is destined to a high calling.

The Protevangelium has therefore invented nothing. Taking this threefold example of the Bible, it has compressed the circumstances peculiar to the birth of Mary into the traditional mould of the "birth of the saints." It must be said at once that it is quite normal for actual events to be recast, without losing their identity, into ready-made literary forms. There are not many different ways in which a newspaper describes a fire, but it does not follow that because the actual event has been so similarly described by various journalists it never took place. The objective truth of a story is not called in question because it is cast in a previously existing literary form.

However, the Protevangelium, no more than the Bible, does not intend to relate objectively the historical facts it makes use of in an ordered and detailed succession; it draws up a "sacred" history, and from the pattern that it uses to mould events there emerges a lesson.

In this narrative three features strike us: the holiness of Mary's parents, God's providential intervention in the birth of the child, and the exceptional destiny that awaits her. Joachim and Anne are undoubtedly of those "holy ones" whom God tests as he did Abraham and Sara, Elcana and Anna and Zachary and Elizabeth. God looks upon the holiness of the parents and we may presume that it will be reflected in their offspring, that Mary will be the fruit of holiness and will be included in the long line of the "just ones" of the Old Testament.

And her birth has a miraculous element. The God of Israel is one who gives fruitfulness and life at his good pleasure. Mary, like Isaac, Samuel and John the Baptist, is one of the free gifts of Providence. In her case, as in theirs, impotent nature has been healed by an omnipotent God.

Under these conditions the child is called upon to play an important rôle in God's plan for man. Isaac was the heir of the divine promise; Samuel was the first of the prophets: what will Mary be? We shall know in due course; but there can be no doubt that consecrated as she was from her mother's womb and born by divine assistance, she is to have some sublime destiny.

The Protevangelium gives us this first lesson: God has displayed all his power at the cradle of her whom he destined for the high honour of becoming the Mother of the Messiah. And this lesson gives unquestionable evidence of the devotion to Mary at the beginning of the second century. For the Christians of whom the Protevangelium is the spokesman Mary is already the "Blessed Virgin," venerated by the Church today. The history of her birth proves that the primitive Christian community had from the outset placed our Lady in the category of the greatest saints.

We must not expect that our author could have then perceived Mary's pre-eminent sanctity, or her immaculate purity. Time had to elapse before the reflection of the Christian mind could realize that the Virgin was the woman preserved from all stain from her mother's womb that she might bring forth Christ. When the Church proclaimed the dogma of the Immaculate Conception of Mary she had allowed the mystery of the Virgin Mother to develop during the Centuries. Scripture had led the Church to the conclusion that Mary had been destined by God from all eternity to be the Mother of his Son. How could she give God himself to the world without sharing in Christ's privilege of being free from all sin (John 8. 46)? All women when they bring children to birth pass on to them an inheritance of original sin, which has passed from Adam and Eve to all the human race, their descendants (Romans 5. 12). Mary, if she was to beget the Son of God all sinless, must therefore be herself immaculately conceived. She was redeemed antecedently, by the power of the blood of that Christ whom it was her office to prepare for his work of salvation.

Popular devotion of the early Church, if it could not penetrate the depths of this mystery, yet had an insight into it. Mary was born of holy parents: she was consecrated to God from her birth, and her birth from a barren mother was in itself miraculous. This pious narrative, based on Scripture, is an illustration of the primitive faith in the "original sanctity" of Mary. A much later edition of the Protevangelium in the tenth century contrived to bring the full implications of all this by the statement:

> When God closes the womb he does so to open it again in a more wonderful way, so that we may understand that the one thus born is not the offspring of passion or sin, but a gift from God. [And the "Book of the Birth of Mary" concludes:] And so in due course, as she was herself born miraculously of a barren woman, she in turn by an incomparable miracle, while remaining a virgin, brought into the world the Son of the Most High, the Saviour of the World. (de *Nat. Mar.* 3. 1, 3.).

This is what we believe also. God prepared mankind for the supreme miracle of the Virgin birth by the lesser miracle of the fruitfulness of the holy women. In the divine plan, Sara, Anna the mother of Samuel, and Elizabeth prefigured Mary herself in her virginal birth.

CHAPTER III

MARY'S GIRLHOOD

The Protevangelium narrates only certain incidents in Mary's childhood, destined to show her unusual maturity and great purity. Thus, at an early age she began to walk: "When she was six months old, her mother stood her up to see if she could stand. She walked seven steps and then returned to her mother's lap" (Prot. 6. 1).

The child soon gave evidence of an unusual self-command. Surely it was a sign from heaven that she should lose no time in following the course which God had marked for her. Her parents recalled that they had vowed to consecrate her to God "all the days of her life." In what way should this be carried out? Without waiting further, Anne erected an "oratory" in the child's bedchamber, where she praised God as in a child's sanctuary, in the company of many young virgins, who were the guardians of her innocence. The childhood of Mary was thus preserved from evil influences and she kept her virginal innocence. The child did not delay in ratifying in the most public way her consecration to God. And so we come to the famous and charming incident of her Presentation in the Temple.

MARY'S PRESENTATION IN THE TEMPLE

When she was just three years old, the child left her family and was consecrated to God in the Temple, where she was to remain in his service for the rest of her life. It was a touching moment: Anne and Joachim were all eagerness to see whether Mary could fulfil the vow they made in her name before she was born.

Certainly the child was young to live away from her parents; they were concerned at this, but Mary, mature as she already was, found a way of proclaiming before all her personal devotion. And this is how she did it. She was led to the Temple by a company of young virgins; she did not glance back at her parents, but went straight on, fixing her eyes on the flames of the candles carried by all in the procession. Her whole bearing thus expressed her inward devotion. This was the crucial moment. The procession moved on. We are reminded of the Parable of the Wise Virgins, who enter into the Bridal Chamber to enjoy the wedding for eternity (Matt. 25. 1-13). Surely Mary was to show herself as supremely the *Virgo sapiens*?

Pseudo-Matthew tells us quite simply: "Mary ran up the fifteen steps of the altar without looking back and seeking her parents as little children are wont to do" (Ps-Matt. 4. 1). A remarkable indication of her early maturity and proof of her entire devotion. At this, all recognized in Mary a privileged servant of God. In the sanctuary of the Temple "the priest took the child up in his arms and blessed her with the words 'The Lord hath magnified thy name among all generations, and the Lord shall manifest in thee in later days his redemption of the children of Israel' " (Prot. 7. 2).

After these prophetic announcements, heralding Mary's own Magnificat, the priest "made her sit on the third step of the altar. And the Lord came upon her with his grace and she danced with her feet . . ." (Prot. 7.3). It is the solemn moment of her consecration. In ancient times dancing was not a profane act, but an expression of prayer. David, a King after God's own heart, had danced by the

Ark of the Covenant in Yahweh's presence, to express the joy he felt in the divine presence (II Kings 6. 5, 21). And here is the point of the whole story: "And her parents returned from the Temple marvelling and praising God because the child had not looked back. And Mary abode in the Temple" (Prot. 8. 1).

The final remark undoubtedly reminds us of the earlier story of the infant Samuel. We have already noticed how the first Anna's son was vowed to God in very similar circumstances to the present. He also, when just weaned, was taken to the Temple (I Kings 1. 22). It is not to be imagined that he took this step quite as spontaneously as did Mary, but when his parents returned, Samuel "remained to minister, at the bidding of the priest Heli, in the Lord's presence" (I Kings 2. 11). And to emphasize that the child in spite of his extreme youth could undertake this sacred office, the sacred narrative tells us: "still as he grew he advanced in favour both with God and with man" (I Kings 2. 26).

The apocryphal writings have faithfully followed their prototype. Mary has not only been "presented" in the Temple, she is confided to its keeping to fulfil her mother's vow, modelled most possibly on that which Anna made for Samuel: "I make a grant of him to the Lord, a grant that shall be as long as his life" (I Kings 1. 27).

THE CONSECRATED LIFE

Thus from her earliest childhood, Mary had on her own account ratified her parents' vow. And we shall not be surprised to find that she is completely at home in God's house. A single sentence from the Protevangelium shows her apart in deep communing with God: "Mary dwelt in the Temple of the Lord, like a dove, and she received food from the hand of an angel" (Prot. 8. 1).

This information was considered too meagre, and there was considerable curiosity to know what she did in the Temple. Pseudo-Matthew shows her living just as a perfect nun in her convent. Mary, he says, "gave herself so completely to the praise of God, that no one would have taken her for a child but a grown up: She prayed at great length as if she was thirty" (Ps-Matt. 6. 1). A rule of life, we learn, governed this cloistered existence, and the long hours of prayer were only broken by weaving, and even when the angel brought her food she did not cease her prayer.

These rather naïve intimations perhaps make us smile, but we ought to perceive the depth of insight they contain.

Among her adopted companions Mary was considered, we are told, as an example of every perfection: "No one showed themselves more attentive at the watches (of prayer), more learned in the law of God than she, or more humble, more eager to sing the psalms of David, more courteous in charity, more outstanding in chastity, and in all virtues most perfect; she was strong, unshakeable, persevering, and every day progressed in perfection" (Ps-Matt. 6. 2).

To round off his picture of the perfect religious in her convent pseudo-Matthew has fallen into a grave anachronism, for it was only in the fourth century of the Christian era that religious communities of women were instituted. So it is obvious that when our author took up his pen towards the sixth century (at the time when the Latin West experienced a striking flowering of the monastic life) he pictured Mary as a nun so as to hold her up the first and greatest model for the nuns of his own time.

But still, beneath these debatable circumstances, to which we shall later return,[1] the author does suggest some

[1] On the subject of Mary's vow of Virginity.

deep truths. Does not Mary in the Gospel show a deep intimacy with God when she receives her word, saying "behold the handmaid of the Lord." To be "in the service" of the Lord reveals a complete submission to his will, which can only be the fruit of prolonged and frequent prayer. St Luke has depicted Mary as of a definitely contemplative nature; it is so to say the refrain of his Gospel: "but Mary up treasured all these sayings, and reflected on them in her heart" (Luke 2. 19).

Would it be too hazardous to maintain that such a continued habit of prayer argues a long training? What we know of the customs of her time confirms us in the idea that Mary had received a very careful religious training. Young Jews early learnt to read and meditate on the Scriptures: in the schools attached to the synagogue the young were instructed in the Law of Moses and the prophets and frequently taken to the Temple for the liturgical prayers. Jewish worship had at that time a daily regularity of an almost monastic character.[2] And it cannot be questioned that Mary supremely among the girls of Israel had excelled in the practices of her ancestral religion, otherwise how can we explain her spontaneous answer to the expression of the divine will in her regard.

The apocryphal writings have thus brought Mary into the Temple, and from her earliest years turned her into a nun. Did their authors perceive that this was an unusual and highly unlikely situation? In the first place the Blessed Virgin was to leave her "cloister" one day to be betrothed to Joseph. This at least the Gospel text demands. Further, however little the customs of the period are known to us, was there ever a case of a girl being presented in the

[2] The day was divided by the hours of prayer and sacrifices in the Temple every three hours. "At the third hour" (9 a.m.), "at the sixth hour" (mid-day), and "the ninth hour" (3 p.m.) we see the apostles going up to the Temple (Acts 3.1).

Temple and allowed to pass her days in the company of
the priests? On this point Jewish custom was decisive:
boys alone could be consecrated to the service of the
sanctuary. The Bible itself only mentions one case of a
consecration to the Temple service, that of the young
Samuel, which is largely the basis for the apocryphal
stories about Mary. So we have an instance of literary
transposition.

In addition, Mary was a child when Herod was rebuild-
ing the Temple of Jerusalem between 20-10 B.C. Mary
would have been about ten when the new building was
completed, and it was only from this age that she could
have begun to frequent the sanctuary. Then, too, it must be
borne in mind that Mary, according to the Gospel, did not
live in Jerusalem but in "a city of Galilee called Nazareth"
(Luke 1. 26). In any case it was there that the angel
found her when she was about sixteen. Most probably she
went up to the Temple with her parents in one of those
pilgrimages to Jerusalem from the provinces. The idea of
the "Presentation," and of a prolonged stay in the Temple
was no doubt suggested to the apochryphas by many biblical analogies. Besides the story of Samuel (I Kings 1-2)
which would form their basis, we may imagine that they
also made use of the Gospel theme of the "Presentation
of Jesus in the Temple," in which we see an old prophetess
Anna who lived in the precincts of the Temple: "who
abode continually in the Temple night and day, serving
God with fasting and prayer" (Luke 2. 37).

But it is just possible that, anticipating a profound in-
tuition of the Christian liturgies, the Protevangelium and
pseudo-Matthew have attributed to Mary what in the Old
Testament had been attributed to Wisdom personified:
"in his own holy dwelling-place I waited on his presence"
(Eccles 24. 14).

This single verse may be the inspiration of our authors and be the origin of the edifying story of Mary's stay in the Temple. In this case we have here an example of what we have called an abuse of the midrash method; it would be, then, a purely scriptural transposition which makes Mary, like Samuel and personified Wisdom, an inhabitant of the divine sanctuary.

But however fanciful it may appear, this pious story does bring out a profound truth: Mary, whose childhood gave promise of such a unique future, must enter early into this "divine exchange" which would prepare her for the highest union. If she was to be one day herself the Temple of God, ought she not to be brought up in the shadow of the sacred building? This at least is the picture which the first Christian generations had of our Lady.

THE VOW OF VIRGINITY

The Protevangelium and pseudo-Matthew after describing Mary's birth and her nunlike life in the Temple should at least have in common some incident based on the Gospel of St Luke, to which they set out to be the preface. Now, in the Gospel narrative when Mary appears for the first time, we are told that she was a virgin betrothed to a man called Joseph (Luke 1. 26-7). How have our authors harmonized the idea of the cloistered life with the betrothal? We must go back to the narrative, and this is what we are told. When Mary was twelve years old the council of priests who had charge of her since her entry met to decide on her: "Behold Mary is become twelve years old in the sanctuary of the Lord. What then shall we do with her lest she pollute the sanctuary of the Lord?" (Prot. 8. 2). The scruple of the priests is understandable; the young girl had arrived at the age of puberty, and according to the Jewish Law a girl when she reached the age of puberty defiled the Temple.[3] It was then the divine intention that Mary should leave the Temple and a husband for her was sought. We may be surprised at this abrupt change of plan, yet it is perfectly understandable. Mary could no longer remain in the Temple, because she is ritually unclean: she has already arrived at a marriageable age, for girls marry very young in the East.[4]

The girl was now ripe for marriage. But what of her "conventual" past? The Protevangelium seems to forget very quickly that her mother had vowed her "to serve the Lord all the days of her life." Incredible as it is, the author does not refer to it.

More logically, pseudo-Matthew puts the problem clearly: has Mary been created for the purpose of marriage? Has she not a higher vocation which she is bound to fulfil, both by virtue of her mother's vow before her birth, and also of her own personal dedication? And this is how the author, four hundred years after the events he was describing, portrays Mary's attitude to her destiny:

> Now it came to pass, that she attained the age of fourteen so that the Pharisees[5] found occasion to say that the time had come for obedience to the custom that no woman of that age should abide in the Temple of God. [The High Priest called the people together, and addressed them thus:] Hear me, O sons of Israel, and receive my word into your ears! Ever since this Temple was built by Solomon, there have been in it virgins, the daughters of kings and the daughters of prophets, and of high priests and of priests:

[3] In the old Hebrew codes bodily defilements, "ritual" as they were called, rendered the subject unsuitable for the worship of the "God of holiness" (cf. Lev. 15. 25-30).

[4] Jewish inscriptions found at Rome, dating from the earliest Christian times, tell of a certain Sabina, a widow of eighteen after three years of marriage, and a Margaret, died at nineteen, after four years of marriage (cf. *Corpus des Inscriptions Juives.* Frey.).

[5] Jews who were excessively scrupulous and exacting in their observance of the Law: they came into conflict with Christ by their intransigent attitude to its literal observance.

they were great and worthy of admiration. But when they
came to the proper age they were given in marriage and
followed the course of their mothers before them and were
pleasing to God. But one alone, Mary, has found a new
way of pleasing God; she has promised to remain a virgin.
(Ps-Matt. 8. 1).

This is the first time that the matter has been mentioned
openly. Contrary to the tradition prevailing until then
Mary has made a vow of virginity; she has bound herself
to take no other spouse than God himself. Pseudo-Matthew informs us how the idea of this vow came to the
young girl's mind. The high priest, he says, had attempted
several times to give his own son to her in marriage. "But
Mary opposed this, saying: it cannot be that I should know
a man." [6]

When all her relations kept answering: "God is worshipped in children and honoured in posterity," Mary
firmly rejoined: "God is worshipped in chastity first of all."
(Ps-Matt. 7. 1). And she quotes the examples of the
patriarch Abel and the prophet Elias to clinch the matter:
"Now I, from my infancy in the Temple of God, have
learnt that virginity can be sufficiently dear to God. And
so because I can offer what is dear to God, I have resolved in my heart that I should not know a man at all"
(Ps-Matt. 7. 2).[7]

Pseudo-Matthew in the sixth century has no doubt
whatever: Mary has made a vow of virginity. She made
it of her own accord before the "angel of the annunciation"
came to reveal to her the deeper mystery of this engagement.

[6] "To know a man" means in Jewish terminology to have sexual
intercourse with a man. This taken here from Luke 1. 34.

[7] This is the second time that Mary freely and in an affirmative
sense repeats the question put to the Angel at the annunciation
regarding her conception: "How can that be, since I have no knowledge of man?" (Luke 1.34).

DID MARY VOW HERSELF TO VIRGINITY BEFORE THE ANNUNCIATION?

This is a question which the historian of Christian origins will ask himself, and today everyone who wishes to understand more profoundly the mystery of Mary. It is usual to maintain that Mary did not wait for the angel's visit announcing her virginal motherhood to make her vow of virginity. It is said that she made this vow when quite young. The oldest traditions that we have indicate this, though they show that some evolution of the early belief on this subject has taken place.

We must not fail to notice that the Protevangelium, at the beginning of the second century, does not speak of a "vow of virginity" by Mary. Certainly Anne had promised to consecrate her child to God for life. But Mary did not consider that she was bound to any definite "state of life" by this promise and her upbringing in the Temple. At the time of adolescence it was the normal thing for the priests to return the girl to the world and seek a husband for her.

It was only four hundred years later, in the sixth century that the pseudo-Matthew, adopting his sources, stated that Mary made an express vow of virginity, to "preserve her chastity," and rejected all offers of marriage. This she did of her own accord, before a revelation from heaven showed her that it was supremely in agreement with the divine plan.

We have already indicated how the author arrived at this view. He had striven to show Mary as the perfect nun in a convent: and how he would make her the first—and the model—of consecrated virgins. He admitted, of course, that for her own times Mary's was an exceptional case: in vowing perpetual virginity she had created "a new manner of pleasing God."

This was certainly a bold innovation. Religious houses
of women did not exist before the fourth century and the
formal, public vow of virginity did not exist previous to
this.

Yet the question remained. If Mary could not pronounce the formal monastic "vow" of virginity, at least
interiorly she could make a "private promise" of virginity,
which would be its hidden equivalent. This is the question
under discussion. Some think that Mary had definitely
undertaken, even if it were only by private promise, to
preserve her virginity: others maintain that this was impossible for Mary until the angel revealed to her that she
was to remain a virgin to become the mother of the
Messiah.

These opinions are freely discussed in the Church, and
today are very much in the air. Why is this? Because they
do not impinge on the one matter of faith in this question,
namely, that Mary was indeed a virgin in giving birth to
Christ.

WHAT THE GOSPEL SAYS

As the starting point of our problem we find a verse of
the Bible which leaves no room for doubt. In the account
of the annunciation in St Luke (1. 26-38) the angel reveals to Mary that she is to be the Mother of the Messiah,
and she asks: "How can that be, since I have no knowledge of man?" (verse 34).

One thing emerges clearly from these words: Mary
states that she *is* a virgin; she has no idea of conjugal
relations with any man. But does this mean, as some hold
that the present tense "I have no knowledge of man"
means, "I have decided not to know," that is, "I wish to
keep my virginity." It is possible, but not certain. The

silence of the Gospel on this matter is the more vexing because it seems to be unaware of any stay of Mary in the Temple. For St Luke the beginning is the moment when Mary is "a virgin betrothed" to Joseph (Luke 1. 27). We shall now try to throw some light on this problem.

A MATTER OF JEWISH HISTORY

We turn now to history. Could a Jewish maiden like Mary desire the life of virginity? A study of the law and the ancestral customs of Israel shows that this was hardly possible. Jewish tradition insisted that girls should marry as soon as they reached marriageable age. The reason is clear: the Chosen People read in the Bible that the supreme promise of God was to give it a numerous posterity. See, for instance, the promise made to Abraham the Father of the people (Gen. 15. 1-6). And also every young Jewess hoped that the Messiah would be born of her, and so they set about the business of marriage as early as possible. No greater trial could befall them than to be sterile or die unmarried, without knowing the blessing of marriage and fecundity. This is the reason why, throughout the Old Testament, we do not find that any Jewish girls spontaneously chose the state of virginity in order to please God. Admittedly in the time of Christ there was a certain movement among the fervent élite of the Jews in favour of virginity. But this trend, which Christianity was later to develop, was still in the time of Mary very much in an embryonic state.

Would our Lady have been quite uninfluenced by the manners and customs of her race and her time? Before answering this question with the help of all the latest historical discoveries, we must admit that the traditional sources give rather a negative answer. The Gospel, we have already explained, shows Mary as already "betrothed" to a man called Joseph. But it is rather of marriage that we must speak; it is most important to understand that the Jewish betrothal, unlike our own, was at that time equal to marriage: the betrothed were united by a contract which could be broken only by formal repudiation. They were already "husband and wife," though their conjugal relations were different until the solemn introduction of the young woman into her husband's dwelling, a ceremony which sealed the marriage.[8]

When, then, the angel came to Mary she was united to Joseph by a real marriage bond, except for the actual cohabitation. The Gospel affords not the least doubt on this point. St Matthew when he speaks of the betrothed couple calls Joseph "her husband" and Mary "his wife" (Matt. 1. 19-20). And if St Luke prefers "the virgin betrothed" it is because he regards the couple as being still between the engagement contract and formal cohabitation.[9]

In these circumstances it can be asked how Mary, now engaged in marriage, could harbour a desire for virginity. It could be imagined that, like other Jewish women, she would look to motherhood when she received from heaven the revelation that she was to preserve her present virginity to become through the Holy Spirit, the virginal mother of the Messiah (Luke 1. 35). This announcement —a complete change of outlook, could well be disturbing to Mary. But with a faith worthy of all praise the young woman had accepted the divine intimation there and then to remain a virgin as the divine plan had ordained. Her *fiat* (Luke 1. 38) would then be the expression of her

[8] Which is why our Gospels use the term "betrothal" for the period before the final union.

[9] According to Rabbinic law this should not take place less than twelve months after the contract.

decision to remain a virgin so as to give herself wholly to her new calling: to bring into the world, without human intercourse, the Son of God in person.

This opinion which has recently been maintained by a Catholic New Testament scholar[10] is very attractive. It accepts all the Gospel data, while it has the merit of preserving the "marriage" of the virgin in all its historic reality.

WHAT HAS TRADITION TO SAY?

Tradition has also something to add, if only to show that the question is not a recent one. We note first of all that Mary's "vow of virginity" was not discussed before the fourth century. It is from this date that the Fathers of the Church and the theologians have been almost unanimous in maintaining that before the Annunciation Mary made, if not a vow, at least a "firm resolution" to remain a virgin.

After St Ambrose, it is St Augustine who first discusses the matter fully. In his treatise on virginity the great Doctor dwells on the famous verse of St Luke when Mary contends with the angel, and he remarks: "Certainly, she would not speak thus if she had not previously vowed her virginity to God."

His reasoning may be summarized thus: God could intimate to Mary the command to remain a virgin only at the moment of the annunciation, but the Mother of Christ was destined to serve as a model to the holy virgins who would follow after her. To inspire her imitators to act freely and spontaneously, it was fitting that Mary should consecrate herself before the message of the angel. But is this argument convincing? St Augustine, like his succes-

[10] Fr J. P. Audet, O.P. "L'Annonce à Marie" in *Revue Biblique*, 1956, pp. 346-74.

sors, wishes to liken the vows of nuns (whose convents were increasing in his time) to the supreme example of Mary. It is to be feared that this approach—followed by pseudo-Matthew—has somewhat coloured the whole of tradition on this point.

Modern theologians, then, seek for more valid reasons for upholding the traditional opinion. It has been remarked that the case of Mary is an exceptional one, for she was a privileged creature of God. Preserved from all stain at the first moment of conception, her whole life could only pass in a total consecration to God. The ideal of virginity is part and parcel of her perfection. So much so that it can be said: "to deny the resolution of virginity in Mary is to deprive the Mother of the Saviour of something of her virginal perfection" and further: "to maintain that Mary adopted this attitude at the moment of the annunciation, or even afterwards in view of the nature of her maternity, which made it imperative, is to misconceive the perfection of her virginity." [11]

The matter is removed here from the historical or psychological order to that of ontological perfection: it is the very nature of Mary, the holiness of her exceptional being which necessitate that she should be raised above the common law of times and customs, and demands from her an absolute vow, even though private, of virginity.

It could be objected that Mary could have "lived" the state of virginity according to the perfection of her being, without having actually "professed" it. Was she conscious of being a woman "blessed among women" and "full of grace" before the angel revealed to her the mystery of her virginal maternity? "Mary was, indeed, a miracle of grace; but as the Church becomes increasingly aware of this mystery we are able to understand ever more clearly that this

[11] J. Galot, S.J., "Vierge entre les vierges" in *Nouvelle Revue Theologique*, 1957, pp. 463-77.

49

miracle of grace was a life lived in a whole community, in the profundity of faith. . . ."

The nun who wrote this at the end of a serious study of chastity and virginity in the Old and New Testaments[12] concluded by saying "there was no psychological miracle in Mary." This means that if tradition and theology are right in confronting us with the "exceptional ontological case" of Mary, a unique and privileged child of God, it follows that by her psychology the Blessed Virgin was not exempt, it seems, from sharing the general ideas of her time.

RETURN TO THE SOURCES

If verse 34 of the first chapter of St Luke remains enigmatic, there are still learned critics to defend the traditional theory of the vow of virginity.

In an outstanding work[13] Fr R. Laurentin has drawn attention to the context of the verse. The evangelist several times speaks of "the virgin," and seems to insist, as if it were a paradox, upon using the phrase "a virgin betrothed" which is equivalent in fact to "married virgin" (Luke 1. 27). In emphasizing that Joseph's wife, though bound by the bonds of marriage, is yet still a virgin, has not Luke delicately suggested that this quite exceptional state could only have been attained through some earlier secret decision. For according to the Rabbis, it was not uncommon for couples to consummate their marriages secretly rather than wait for the legal day of cohabitation.

On the other hand Fr Stanislaus Lyonnet[14] shows how the very flow of the narrative is only comprehensible if

[12] Sr Jeanne d'Arc: in *Chastity* (London, 1955), p. 19.
[13] *Structure et Théologie de Luc 1-11*. Etudes Bibliques (Paris, 1957), pp. 176-88.
[14] *Le récit de l'Annonciation et de la maternité divine de la Sainte Vierge,* Institut Biblique, Rome, 1956.

Mary objects to the angel that she is firmly resolved to
remain a virgin. Indeed, how could Mary have raised the
matter when hearing of her motherhood, if she had been
bent in the ordinary way upon having children. Her ap-
prehension is explained on the other hand better on the
hypothesis that she had renounced motherhood: the angel
had to make clear to her that so far from being an ob-
stacle to God's design, her virginity was going to be the
special instrument of it: she would be a mother without
man's intervention: the Holy Spirit himself would make
her conceive (Luke 1. 35ff.).

Besides this defence of the traditional view a further
element is added, enlarged upon by the authors whom we
have just cited. It is the light shed by the Dead Sea Scrolls,
discovered ten years ago on the site of Qumran in Palestine. As we know, excavations on the border of Palestine
have brought to light a well stocked library of a monastery
of monks who lived in the first century before and after
Christ. The documents and monastic ruins prove that they
were Essenes. This sect, which had broken away from the
official Jewish religion, retired to the desert and formed
a community with very lofty principles. With prayer, fasting and continuous meditation on the Scriptures they
made ready for the coming of the Messiah.

Among these an elect group practised celibacy.[15] This
was a sufficiently remarkable fact for the period to have
attracted the attention of the great contemporary histori-
ans, Pliny, Flavius Josephus and Philo of Alexandria. The
last-named emphasized clearly how the practice of chastity by these ascetics fostered a community life in which
the love of God held the first place. "The Essenes," he
says, "give numberless indications of the love of God:

[15] Not all the Essenes were celibates: in the cemetery of Qumran
the bones of women and children have been found in the tombs,
though not very often.

such as chastity practised during their whole life, continuously and unbroken." [16] And the same historian tells us also that in another sect at that period there were women who "practised continence, not out of compulsion like various Greek priestesses, but freely, for love of Wisdom." [17]

We cannot be absolutely certain what is signified by the virginity of these women in this Jewish community of Therapeutes, contemporary with Mary: the Dead Sea Scrolls only confirm the practice of celibacy among men. But there is no reason to suspect Philo, generally considered trustworthy, of invention or error in this respect.

All this goes to show that in Mary's lifetime the ideal of virginity was not unknown to a certain élite among Jewish men and women. For a little time past a change was beginning in Judaism: virginity which had hitherto been despised, was now becoming an ideal higher than marriage and the begetting of children.[18] It is not without interest to notice that this ideal grew up among small groups of devout Israelites who confidently awaited the coming of the Messiah. Was Mary in any way influenced by these ideas? When she came to the age of marriage, was she led by the altogether special grace she possessed towards this ideal of Messianic expectation? It is interesting to note that the Gospel presents as close to Mary only men who are chaste; John the Baptist, whose solitary and ascetic life and spirituality resemble those of the Essenes; Joseph especially, who, as we shall see, had the greatest respect for the virginal mystery (or state) of his wife; later John, the beloved Apostle of Christ, selected because

[16] Philo, *The Contemplative Life,* no. 68.
[17] Philo, treatise on *Spiritual Freedom,* quoted by R. Laurentin, op. cit., p. 186-7.
[18] As early as A.D. 56, in the middle of the first century of our era, St Paul vouched for the practice of virginity by women. (1 Cor. 7. 32-8).

he was a virgin, as the guardian of Mary on the death of her Son (John 19. 26-27). Though the Gospel does not state the fact, we may suppose that our Lady wishing to remain a virgin, sought in Joseph a companion filled with the same idea, who would share her secret vow under the protection of marriage.

On these grounds we should find in the case of Mary a situation analogous to that with which the apocryphal books have made us familiar. Yet there is this difference: we do not know the sequence of events. The stay in the Temple is an exaggerated picture, which will not stand historical criticism. But apart from this "monastic" framework, it is now agreed that Mary, quite spontaneously, may have accepted the ideal of virginity. In any case, to conclude this discussion we recall that the Catholic Faith, based on Scripture and Tradition, does not oblige us to hold anything except that Mary, born a virgin, lived as such: the angel found her a virgin, she became, at his word, the virginal mother of our Saviour.

CHAPTER IV

THE MARRIAGE BOND

JOSEPH, THE CHOSEN MAN OF GOD

The Gospel, we may remember, when it speaks of Mary for the first time, shows her as already engaged to be married. She is, according to St Luke: "betrothed to a man of David's lineage: his name was Joseph" (1. 27). How did this meeting, so important in God's plan, come about? We are not told.

This silence the Protevangelium and pseudo-Matthew found perplexing. They did not wish that such an important incident should pass by unnoticed. Had not God most carefully chosen Mary's companion? They emphasized this belief by recounting the episode—a charming one, certainly—of the miraculous wand. It is this.

When the high priest, whose office it was to guide Mary in the choice of a husband, begged for light from on high, he received this answer: "Zacharias, Zacharias, go forth and gather together those that are widowers[1] of the people, and let them bring every man a rod, and to whomsoever the Lord shall show a sign, his wife shall she be" (Prot. 8. 3). Why must the suitors bring a wand? The answer is to be found in a celebrated passage of the Book of Numbers.

When God wished to choose a colleague for Moses in leading the Hebrews through the desert, he directed the

[1] Pseudo-Matthew says merely "those who have no wife" (8. 2).

patriarch to choose in this manner: each chieftain of Israel was to bring a rod with his name written on it and place it in the Tabernacle. The Lord made his choice known by making Aaron's rod sprout. Thus Moses learnt from God who his helper was to be (Num. 17. 6-13).

This ancient judgement is repeated and adapted by the apocryphal writings. All the widowers in Judea, Joseph among them, are invited to present themselves in the Temple, with a staff in their hand; the High Priest took their rods into the Holy of Holies, in God's presence and then gave them back to their owners: "But Joseph received his rod last: and behold, a dove came forth and flew on to the head of Joseph. And the High Priest said: to thee has it fallen to take the virgin of the Lord" (Prot. 9. 1).

On the biblical precedent we should have expected the rod to have blossomed. Why then, did a dove fly forth? This wonder, even more astonishing than the first, seems to recall the Gospel scene of Jesus' baptism. Christ, we remember, was "pointed out" by God to John the Baptist, as being the chosen one of God, when the Holy Spirit came upon him in the form of a dove (Matt. 3. 16-17).

The whole story of the miraculous rod, then, is simply to emphasize that it is by a divine choice that Joseph also has been indicated as Mary's life companion. God himself has made it known before all.

MARY'S GUARDIAN

So far everything seems easy enough: Joseph will be Mary's husband. Husband? Is that certain? Has not his choice destined him for a higher mission? The narrative of the apocryphal writings is here confused. To agree with the Gospel text they have betrothed Joseph and Mary. But this union is in their eyes inconsistent, for they have made quite plain that Mary intends to persevere in her firm intention of consecrating her life to the Lord. So, in their version, Joseph can only refuse a true marriage: he excuses himself from becoming the "husband" of Mary; his vocation is to become the guardian of her virginity: "I am an old man and have sons, why do you entrust this young girl to me?"

It emerges from this passage that the one selected for Mary is not only a widower, but a man advanced in age and in no way anxious for marriage, for he has children already. But he resigns himself to the divine choice: "I do not wish to resist the will of God. I will be this virgin's guardian until God shall make known which of my sons shall take her as wife" (Ps-Matt. 8. 4.).

The Protevangelium is not so categorical. According to it Joseph appears as husband without really being so. So he brings her into his house with these words: "Behold, I have received thee out of the Temple of the Lord: and now I leave thee in my house and I will go away to build my buildings, and I will come again to thee. The Lord shall watch over thee" (Prot. 9. 3).

What a strange way of setting up house! It appears that Joseph does not think of living with his wife: he takes her as a virgin, and goes away to leave her alone to a life of contemplation, such as was hers in the Temple: her new life even though in the state of matrimony, only continues her noviceship as a nun. And so it goes on. As the story continues it shows Mary devoted, in Joseph's house, to the occupations of a vestal. The priests, who remained her real tutors, directed her to weave a precious veil for the sanctuary. We see her passing her days just as she did in the Temple.

It must be frankly admitted that the apocryphal writings, faithful to the religious vocation which they have ascribed to Mary, continue to see in her a virgin consecrated to God alone, and she does not desert that state when she enters Joseph's house. She is a spotless virgin whom the priests have entrusted to a man who, by his age and position, cannot really be her husband, but only her protector. We notice that the Protevangelium, which had not made Mary take a vow of virginity, has yet put these words into the mouth of the priest who entrusted her to Joseph: "To you it has fallen to take the Virgin of the Lord under your care" (Prot. 9. 1).

What is the historical value of the story? According to the Gospel we know that although Mary and Joseph were united in the matrimonial state they were to await the legal time of cohabitation. In fact, when we read St Matthew, it is obvious that Joseph did not straightway take his wife into his house: there was an interval of time, long enough for the carpenter to find that Mary was "with child, by the power of the Holy Ghost" (Matt. 1. 18). It was only when this mystery was explained to him that Joseph was willing to take his wife to himself (Matt. 1. 24). According to the Law, this introduction finally sealed the betrothal and allowed conjugal relations.

Contrary to this, the apocryphal writings bring Mary immediately into the house of her reputed husband: a clear indication of a quite special case: Mary passes into Joseph's care as a virgin handed over to a guardian. There was a practice, which seems to have arisen in the second century, and which lasted until the institution of monasticism, by which a girl who had made a vow of chastity and could not remain with her parents, should ask for the protection and hospitality of one of the opposite sex also vowed to chastity. This practice, known under the Latin name of *virgines subintroductae,* provided the Protevangelium with an excellent model for the celibate union of Joseph and Mary.

Even if these ideas are not so very far removed from

the historical conditions of the first century, according to which it was not unthinkable for a Jewish woman who had made a profession of virginity to seek to put herself under the legal protection of a man inspired with the same ideal, it is clear that in the apocryphal writings the union of Joseph and Mary loses all sense of that deep reality that it has in the Gospel. There is nothing mysterious: the betrothed have contracted no marriage. Their life together is more like the adoption of a girl by an elderly father of a family.

When the time of childbirth comes upon Mary, he was, as we shall see, greatly embarrassed in explaining his relationship to her, and can only answer the question as to whether he is her husband in words which have a Sibylline ring: "Mary is she who was brought up in the Lord's Temple: I received her as a wife by lot: but she is not my wife, and has conceived by the Holy Ghost" (Prot. 19. 1).

CHAPTER V

THE ANNUNCIATION
OF THE VIRGINAL
MOTHERHOOD

The apocryphal writings intimated that when the Virgin Mary was entrusted to Joseph she was destined for a higher union than that of marriage. They could now approach the subject of Mary's Virginal Motherhood.

THE ANNUNCIATION TO MARY

While Joseph was absent on his carpenter's work, Mary spent her days in the old man's house as quietly as in a cloister. There it was that she received the angel's message. This is how it came to pass:

> Mary took the pitcher and went forth to fill it with water. Then a voice was heard: hail, thou art full of grace, the Lord is with thee, thou art blessed among women. And she looked round to the right and to the left, to see where this voice came from. Filled with trembling she went back to the house and took up the purple and sat down and drew out the thread. (Prot. 11. 1).

This charming little episode cannot fail to touch us. It puts the supernatural encounter of the biblical narrative in a pastoral setting. It was at a fountain that Isaac's servant found "Rebecca, the daughter of Bathuel, (who) came out with a pitcher on her shoulder. A maiden most beautiful, fair of face, and a virgin that had no knowledge of man" (Gen. 24. 15-6).

It was also at Jacob's well that Christ revealed himself to the Samaritan woman (John 4). But for the author of the Protevangelium, this country scene is only an introduction. The voice which Mary hears does not reveal its identity, nor the core of its message. Frightened by this mysterious greeting Mary quickly returns to her house and continues her work. Artists often used to take the theme of this visit to the well to show Mary occupied in stitching the purple, the pitcher at her feet.

> And behold an angel of the Lord stood before her saying: Fear not, Mary, for thou hast found favour before the Lord of all things and it is of his word that thou shalt conceive. And she questioned in herself and said: Shall I conceive of the living God, and bring forth after the manner of women? And the angel of the Lord said: Not so, Mary, for the power of the Lord shall overshadow thee: wherefore that Holy Thing that is born of thee shall be called the Son of the Highest. And thou shalt call his name Jesus: for he shall save his people from their sins. And Mary said: behold the handmaid of the Lord, be it done unto me according to thy word. (Prot. 11. 2-3).

Compare this narration with its model in the Gospel (Luke 1. 26-38); the literary and doctrinal inferiority strikes us at once. St Luke, whose word picture is full of charm, has sacrificed nothing of the deeper values as he describes the annunciation. In his masterpiece there is nothing excessive, no distracting details. Everything leads up to the dialogue between Mary and her heavenly visitor. No sooner has he appeared than straightway, with no extraneous details, he states his message. As the event takes place inside a house, what was Mary doing at the time?

Such a detail has no interest for Luke, who is only interested in the message itself: that a Saviour is to be born.

The Protevangelium, on the other hand, piles up the scenic details, and dwells on Mary's reactions. Twice the heavenly voice is heard; at first at the well, then in the house. Obviously it was desired to emphasize the terror felt by Mary at the sound of the voice, while Luke was content to indicate her interior emotion: "She was much perplexed at hearing him speak so, and cast about in her mind what she was to make of such a greeting" (Luke 1. 29).

Why should this perfectly understandable emotion be changed into a panic by the Protevangelium more especially since from her earliest years it has shown her accustomed to familiar converse with angels? As we have seen, the evangelist goes straight to the heart of the angel's message, and this is the announcement of the birth of the Messiah. The whole point of the divine envoy's message is to make known to Mary that she has been chosen by God to bring into the world the Saviour. It is only towards the end (v. 35ff.) that the angel touches upon Mary's question, the miraculous manner of this birth. And how discreetly he tells her that her virginity will be preserved: "The Holy Spirit will come upon thee, and the power of the Most High will overshadow thee. Thus this holy offspring of thine shall be known for the Son of God . . . nothing can be impossible with God" (Luke 1. 35-7).

It is quite otherwise with the more popular and less doctrinal version of the Protevangelium. The centre of interest of the dialogue is abruptly displaced. The announcement of Christ's birth is merely an opportunity to linger over the manner of its realization. The principal concern is the angel's explanation of how Mary can remain a virgin in childbirth.

Mary is first concerned to know if she must have intercourse according to the law of nature. A natural question, to which the angel answers: "No, but through the Word of God." But much more important for pseudo-James is the question which follows: "Shall I really conceive of the living God, and bring forth after the manner of all other women?"

The question which chiefly seems to worry Mary is not to know whether her motherhood will be divine or not, but whether her childbearing will impair her virginity. The apocryphal writings are obsessed with this point—at all costs the physical inviolability of Mary must be preserved. The child is born through a miracle of purity. From her cradle she has been set apart to preserve her chastity intact. She was entrusted to Joseph as she grew to adolescence for no other purpose than to ensure that she should know no defilement. It remained to show that her bodily integrity was carefully safeguarded during her confinement. We shall see later how the author has contrived a narrative of the "immaculate confinement" of Mary. Not only did she conceive through the power of God, but her chastity was unquestionably established in her delivery.

How far has the story in the Protevangelium moved away from the Gospel narrative! For St Luke it is the messianic character that is essential: it is not too much to say that it is Christ who is the most present in his mind in the dialogue of the angel with Mary. The apocryphal writer on the other hand fixes his intention on Mary and the manner of her divine childbirth. The means are taken for the end itself. His curiosity is directed far more towards the physical aspect (bodily integrity) than the moral (virginity of the heart) aspect of this mystery of Mary. And this is the beginning: as the narrative proceeds it is obvious that the interior dispositions of Mary mean much less to him than the miraculous preservation of her bodily purity.

THE VISIT TO ELIZABETH

In St Luke (1. 39-56) Mary's visit in haste to her cousin Elizabeth immediately after the annunciation is for a quite definite purpose. As a result of the angel's last words Mary was anxious to go and establish that "with God nothing is impossible" since her cousin, although old and barren, was herself to have a child (Luke 1. 36-7). Also this early encounter of Jesus with John the Baptist was an intimation that the time was almost at hand when Jesus would open the Kingdom of Heaven.

There appears to be no reason why these motives, which endow the event with special meaning, have completely disappeared in the Protevangelium. Indeed in it Mary, having hastened to the hill country, receives there the greetings fitting for the Mother of the Messiah; but she does not understand them, and seems to have forgotten all about the recent message of the angel. Here is the strange passage:

> And Mary, all jubilant, went away to her cousin Elizabeth. She knocked at the door, and when Elizabeth heard it she cast down the scarlet wool and ran to open it. And when she saw Mary, she blessed her and said: Whence is this to me that the Mother of my Lord should come to me? . . . And Mary forgot the mysteries which the archangel Gabriel had told her, and she looked up into heaven and said: "Who am I, Lord, that all the generations of the earth should bless me? (Prot. 12. 2).

It is strange that Mary should forget her divine Motherhood so soon after she has accepted the angel's message. Perhaps it is only a literary device to bring out more clearly her great humility; she was amazed at the honours to be paid to her in all times and places. But Mary's conduct in the Gospel is much truer to life. Deeply conscious, and how rightly, of the mystery of which she is the subject she is not astonished at the reverence to be paid to her down the ages: she knows that she is the Messiah's Mother and her humility does not suffer thereby for she ascribes all the merit to God: "Behold, from this day forward all generations will count me blessed: because he who is mighty, he whose name is holy has wrought for me his wonders" (Luke 1. 49). In addition, the apocryphal writer concludes this charming scene with a detail whose crude realism is in sharp contrast with the habitual delicacy of St Luke: "And she abode three months with Elizabeth, and day by day her womb grew; and Mary was afraid and departed to her house and hid herself from the children of Israel. Now she was sixteen years old when these mysteries came to pass" (Prot. 12. 3).

CHAPTER VI

THE MOTHERHOOD
AND VIRGINITY OF
MARY

JOSEPH'S FEARS

The Gospel faithfully reflects the consequences of the annunciation. The mystery of Jesus' conception for the moment clouds the perfect union of Joseph and Mary.

It is St Matthew who tells of St Joseph's reactions. Only Mary herself knew of the action of the Holy Spirit in her: Joseph was totally unaware of it. This is how he learnt of it:

> His mother Mary was espoused to Joseph, but they had not yet come together, when she was found to be with child, by the power of the Holy Ghost. Whereupon her husband Joseph (for he was a right-minded man, and would not have put her to open shame) was for sending her away in secret. But hardly had this thought come to his mind, when an angel of the Lord appeared to him in a dream, and said, Joseph, Son of David, do not be afraid to take thy wife Mary to thyself, for it is by the power of the Holy Ghost that she has conceived this child. [Warned in a dream:] Joseph . . . did as the angel of the Lord had bidden him, taking his wife to himself. (Matt. 1. 18-20, 24).

It was perfectly natural that Mary's husband should be disturbed when he found that she was pregnant before their cohabitation. Adultery was common enough among the Jews, yet we can only admire the wise conduct of the man whom the Gospel surnames the "Just." Were his suspicions of Mary quite like those of an ordinary husband? He knew the faith of her whom he had married: he shared with her this ideal of virginity which we must suppose had united them. How could he treat Mary inconsiderately?

The Protevangelium is well aware of the scruple of conscience of this upright soul, but instead of evincing Joseph's discreet reticence it endows this intimate self-searching with a highly dramatic turn. In this account it was in the sixth month—when she could no longer conceal her condition—that Joseph is suddenly confronted with Mary. We must not forget that he had been away since the time he brought her to his house, and had left her to her devout occupations. So it was less as a husband than as guardian of her virginity that the old man became aware of her condition. In a first movement of emotion he rightly blames himself. Has he not neglected his duty of guardianship by his long absence? "With what countenance shall I look unto the Lord my God? What prayer shall I make, concerning this maiden? For I received her as a virgin from the Lord's Temple, but I have not kept her a virgin" (Prot. 13. 1). But after this avowal he inveighs bitterly against the presumed seducer of Mary: "Who has tricked me? Who has committed this crime in my house and defiled this Virgin?" (Prot. ibid.). Our author does not seem to think he is wanting in delicacy in representing the distressing scene in which the old man informs the young girl of his suspicions:

And Joseph called Mary and said to her: O thou who wast cared for by the Lord, what hast thou done? Why hast thou humbled thy soul, thou who wast brought up in the Holy of Holies. . . . But she wept bitterly, saying: I am pure, and do not know any man. And Joseph said to her: Whence then is that which is in thy womb? And she said: As the Lord lives, I do not know whence it came to me (Prot. 13. 2-3).

Strangely we are taken back to the unawareness of her state which Mary, quite forgetfully, had declared to Elizabeth. On his side Joseph reflects on the line of conduct he should adopt. And here we must pay tribute to the Protevangelium for the insight into the psychology of a pious Jew, such as Joseph was, which it shows. For him the dilemma was a cruel one. "If I hide her sin, I gravely disobey the Law of the Lord. But if I reveal her to the children of Israel, I fear lest that which is in her be the seed of an angel, and I shall be found delivering innocent blood to death" (Prot. 14. 1).

Jewish law prescribed capital punishment for a virgin who allowed herself to be seduced before marriage and for adultery. And it was a moral obligation for an obedient Jew to denounce such a crime. One doubt held Joseph back from obeying the Law. If Mary had conceived of an angel he would be delivering an innocent person to death. Where did he get this idea of Mary's intercourse with a heavenly being? First of all, no doubt, from her Temple background, where she had spoken familiarly with heavenly messengers. But also the popular literature of later Judaism gave colour to the possibility of angels making human beings pregnant. The Bible had told how the "Sons of God," that is the angels, had come down to marry the "daughters of men" (Gen. 6. 1-4). Certainly they were bad angels who gave birth to the giants of antiquity: God in his anger had destroyed this first human race in the Flood. But later ages had recognized that human nature could be impregnated immediately by the divine Power.[1]

[1] These intimations of an Incarnation are found in the Bible under the image of the fecundity of the Spirit, the personification of the Word of Wisdom.

Though it remained a great mystery the possibility was present to men's minds. The Protevangelium then puts into Joseph's mind that Mary's pregnancy was due to a supernatural origin.

We do not know exactly what were the feelings of Mary's husband. The Gospel emphasizes his wisdom and sense of delicacy. Though the Law obliged Joseph to deliver Mary over to justice, he preferred to do so "secretly." Partly, no doubt, to avoid a public scandal, but also perhaps because he felt that under the external circumstances lay hidden a profound mystery. Joseph appears to have been quite convinced of Mary's innocence. He knew her virtue; he therefore refused to hand over to the process of the Law this mystery which he did not understand.

In the Gospel, as in the apocryphal narrative, God at last lifts the veil of the mystery—for mystery it is—and at a stroke frees Joseph from all torture of soul. This is often called the "annunciation to Joseph." An angel comes to reveal to him Mary's state: the child in her womb is not the result of sin but is the work of the Holy Ghost. Joseph must not carry out his plan of putting her away, but on the contrary must not hesitate to take her to him. For St Matthew the life together of the two then begins, as if there had been no shadow over their union (Matt. 1. 24). For pseudo-Matthew there is a major scandal; a virgin defiled by the very man who ought to have protected her consecration to God.

THE TRIAL BY WATER

The apocryphal writings have not been able to resist describing the very thing which the Gospel tells us was not done. Mary is handed over to the judgement, not of

Joseph, but of the priests who had earlier assumed the guardianship of her virginity.

We have to understand the intentions of the Protevangelium and pseudo-Matthew. Their point of view is always the same: to show from the facts that Mary remained inviolate. Joseph and Mary, through private revelation, now knew how heaven was concerned in these events. They lived together, Joseph no longer leaving her. An emissary of the high priest, happening to come on a visit, noticed Mary's pregnancy; we can guess what followed: "He ran quickly to the High Priest and told him: Joseph who had your confidence has sinned grievously. The priest asked how. He answered: because he has defiled the Virgin whom he took from the Temple: he has secretly consummated the marriage with her and has not declared it to the children of Israel" (Prot. 15. 2).

A priestly inquiry was immediately instituted. It resulted in the arrest of Joseph and Mary. The two suspects were taken to the Temple. There in the presence of God they were publicly judged according to the Law. Joseph was openly accused of having defiled the Virgin entrusted to him, and Mary had to answer to an even worse sacrilege, namely, infidelity to her virginal consecration. The object is quite clear: this double accusation in public was intended to reveal to all the inviolate virginity of Mary and the innocence of her faithful guardian. Pseudo-Matthew presents a picture that is admirable for its purpose. The trial was held openly in the presence of all. All the people were called together: "The whole multitude of Israel collected, so numerous that they could not be counted" (Ps-Matt. 12. 1).

This almost universal audience was meant to show this judgement as the trial of the century. It would seem that the author wanted to convince the greatest number of contemporary adversaries of Christ's virginal conception in

Mary's womb. The Jews refused to accept Mary's virginity. It was a twofold scandal for them that God should become man, and that a woman had not conceived like other women.

At the beginning of the trial Mary is sharply assailed by those who, knowing her past perfectly well, should have defended her: "The priests, neighbours and parents of Mary said to her, weeping, acknowledge thy sin; thou wast as a dove in the Temple of God, and didst receive thy food at the hand of angels" (Ps-Matt. 12. 2).

The questioning led both Mary and Joseph to vindicate their innocence strongly. But it is curious to notice that neither of them referred to the secret revelation which assured both of their innocence. Probably they would have been treated as visionaries. More certainly their silence is portrayed as an appeal to God's intervention, who will not allow his friends to be confounded, rather he will supremely vindicate their blamelessness. And thus we are treated to the following curious episode: "And the priest said: Restore the virgin whom you received from the Temple of the Lord. Joseph wept bitterly. The priest said: I will give you to drink of the water of conviction of the Lord, and it will make your sin plain to you" (Prot. 16. 1). What is this "water of conviction" which will reveal the sin of the guilty? To vindicate justice ancient times used more or less magical rites of great antiquity. To obtain a verdict in a judicial process recourse was had to the "judgement" of God himself by the use of consecrated water. The Jews had adopted this judicial rite in the course of their history. The High Priest is here only applying a command of the Law of Moses by which every woman suspected of adultery should submit to the following test:

> The priest will take up an earthen jar of lustral water into which he will put a handful of dust from the tabernacle floor . . . if it is true that no stranger has bedded

with thee, and thou hast never defiled thyself by forsaking
thy husband's bed, then these baneful waters I have cursed
shall have no power over thee. But if thou hast left thy duty
towards thy husband . . . the Lord make thee a by-word
of all that is accursed. (Num. 5. 11-22).

It was the belief that this bitter drink, in God's name,
would have the power of revealing secret sins. When an
adulterous woman drank it she would be made sterile: her
sexual powers would wither. On the other hand the innocent woman would not be harmed by drinking the mixture.

If the Protevangelium uses this ancient method afresh
it is because it is seen as the "legal" way of involving God
himself in the trial of Joseph and Mary. The author is
deliberately using a scriptural text to support his thesis that
heaven has unmistakably revealed the virginal conception
of Mary. Such is the result of the "trial by water":

> And the priest took the water of conviction and made
> Joseph drink and sent him into the hill-country. And he
> returned whole. And he made Mary also drink and sent her
> also into the hill country. And she returned whole. And all
> the people marvelled, because no sin appeared in them.
> And the priest said: If the Lord God has not made your
> sin manifest, neither do I condemn you. (Prot. 16. 2).

That the High Priest proclaims Joseph and Mary ac-
quitted because God has himself pronounced in their
favour is surely an allusion to the incident in the Gospel
where Jesus confounds the accusers of the adulterous
woman by forgiving her (John 8).

We can discern from this strange scene the author's intention: the "trial" of the two accused turns against their
accusers. The answer has been given, and cannot be gain-
said by those present: God has vindicated the virginity of
Mary even in her pregnancy. Pseudo-Matthew, which always improves upon its predecessor, informs us more fully
of the theological debate about Mary which, in the sixth

century, was still being carried on by the Jews. Even after this striking vindication at which they were present: "Some upheld her holiness while others, out of a bad conscience, continued to accuse her" (Ps-Matt. 12. 4).

Then Mary made this solemn declaration: "As the Lord lives, before whom I stand: I have not known a man, nor shall I ever know man, for from infancy I have made my resolution. In my infancy I made a vow to God to remain chaste, and to live for him alone: it is for him that I wish all my life to remain chaste" (Ps-Matt. 12. 4).

The trial could not have a more fitting conclusion. Like the preceding episode of the bitter water, this little drama could only lead the reader in ancient times to a single conviction: Mary did not lose her virginity in giving birth to the Messiah. On the contrary, it has been unmistakably shown that she continued a virgin even in her pregnancy. The Protevangelium, as early as the beginning of the second century, expressed exactly the belief of the early Church in the virginity of Mary *ante partum,* that is, before the birth.[2] This belief was securely founded on the verse of St Matthew which says that the Virgin and Joseph had no sexual relations after as before their cohabitation. "Joseph . . . did as the angel of the Lord had bidden him, taking his wife to himself, and he had not known her when she bore a son, her firstborn, to whom he gave the name Jesus" (Matt. 1. 24-25). If the apocryphal writers had taken the trouble to read this verse carefully, perhaps they would have been more sparing of a narrative which was, it must be agreed, rather detrimental to Mary and her virtuous husband.

The apocryphal writings set out to tell Mary's life up to the birth of Christ. But as we shall see, it is less the

[2] Cf. in this series Mgr Suenens, *Mary, The Mother of God,* pp. 39-44.

Messiah's entry into the world which interests them than Mary's conduct. The events at which we are going to look all bear on the one question: how was Mary's virginal purity preserved right to the end?

Following the indications furnished by St Luke (2. 1-7) the epic story of Bethlehem is unfolded. As in the Gospel Joseph and Mary are on the way to the little town of Juda where they had to present themselves to be recorded. On the journey Joseph indulges in a monologue which reveals the embarrassment of his matrimonial position: "I will record my sons: but this child (Mary), what shall I do with her? How shall I register her? As my wife? but I am ashamed. Or as my daughter? But all the children of Israel know that she is not my daughter. This day of the Lord (the day of registration) I will do the will of the Lord (as the Lord inspires me) (Prot. 17. 1).

While they are on the journey Mary feels that the time of her delivery is upon her. Reread St Luke. Here he goes straight to the point: the bringing of Jesus into the world. His words breathe an air of freshness and spontaneity: "It was while they were still there that the time came for her delivery. She brought forth a son, her first born, whom she wrapped in his swaddling clothes" (Luke 2. 6-7). Nothing could be clearer. But the Protevangelium did not wish this birth to occur unnoticed, just like any other birth. His intention was that we should be present at the birth to be impressed by its exceptional character. For this end he sees fit to relate to us the following somewhat coarse story.

THE STORY OF THE MIDWIVES

Leaving Mary in a wayside cave with his sons by her, Joseph hurries off to seek a midwife. Quite providentially he meets one. She is a Jewess, and according to pseudo-

Matthew is called Zelomi. She inquires who the woman is who is about to give birth, and Joseph who is always embarrassed by such questions evasively answers "she is my betrothed." Zelomi is surprised: "How is that: is she not your wife?"

To reassure her he explains. "It is Mary, who was brought up in the Temple of the Lord. By lot she was given to me for bride, but she is not my wife. She has conceived through the Holy Spirit" (Prot. 19. 1). The midwife then asks the vital question: "Is this true? can a virgin give birth to a child?"

Joseph brings her to the cave. They are met by a strange sight: a cloud envelops the hollow in the rock. This was traditionally the sign for the Jews of God's Presence among his people. Zelomi has no doubt that God has come down on the place. When she is brought to Mary she is overcome by the strange event: the bright cloud diminishes and vanishes and in its place is the puny figure of the newborn child, Jesus. Joseph relates this marvelous vision: "A great light appeared in the cave so that our eyes could not bear it. And little by little the light withdrew until the infant appeared, and it went and took the breast of its mother, Mary. And then the midwife cried: this is a great day for me, for I have seen a wonderful sight" (Prot. 19. 2). The purpose of this description is to show clearly the supernatural character of the birth. The new-born child "appears" in a heavenly halo, as Yahweh of old in glory. But the Protevangelium has not entirely avoided suggesting to the reader the suspicion that the infant came directly from heaven like a ray of light and not from Mary's womb? This is a plausible view, for the Docetist heresy flourished in the second century, teaching that the Son of God had taken human nature only in appearance. It is true that the author has given such a realistic appearance to Mary's pregnancy that it is difficult to believe that he does not consider that there was a genuine childbirth. The presence of the midwife is an assurance, even though, in fact, she may not have intervened.[3]

The Protevangelium is above all at pains to emphasize that this birth has not been subject to the normal laws of motherhood. A detail will explain what we mean: hardly has the infant been born when he goes to his mother's breast. Is this not a discreet intimation that neither Jesus nor his mother have suffered from the normal defilements of childbirth? When the angel announced to Mary her virginal motherhood, she inquired "Shall I really conceive of the living God, and bring forth like other women?"

As we have remarked, this question prepared the ground for the present narrative. Mary was concerned to know whether her virginity would be preserved in childbirth itself. The "wonderful event" which astonished the midwife so greatly seems to have been precisely Mary's immaculate childbirth. The miracle is clear, both through the coming of the Infant all undefiled and surrounded with a radiance of glory, and by the incident of the mother appearing to escape the penalties of childbirth.

As she came away from such an unusual sight Zelomi met an acquaintance, a midwife like herself. Immediately she told her: "Salome, Salome. I have an unheard of thing to tell you: a virgin has just given birth contrary to all nature!"

Such a statement while provoking curiosity, does not arouse scepticism. The Jews, who were bitter opponents of the virginal conception of Mary, could read in the Bible that a righteous cause must rest upon the deposition of two witnesses. Would Salome add her witness? For the mo-

---

[3] It is not uncommon even today among the Arabs, as it was of old among the Jews, for women to give birth without a midwife. The Gospel certainly does not mention a midwife at Jesus' birth.

ment she was inclined to be incredulous like the Jews. To
Zelomi's spontaneous declaration she opposed her doubt:
"Can this possibly be true?"

It is also the reader's question, and the one which the
Protevangelium sets out to answer from the beginning of
the book. Imitating the scene in the Gospel where the
Apostle Thomas, alone of the twelve, refused to believe in
the resurrection of Jesus (John 20. 24-9), Salome also is
made to demand a tangible proof: "As the Lord liveth, if
I do not touch with my hand and prove her nature I will
not believe than a virgin has brought forth" (Prot. 19. 3).

We are inclined to be surprised at such brazenness. Of
course, the author had scriptural precedents; Thomas
would not believe before putting his fingers into the open
wounds of the Crucified. But the difference here is in extremely bad taste and certainly offensive to modesty. How
could the writer, who is so respectful to Mary, dare to
imagine such an incident: "Salome wished to prove the
nature of Mary with her own hand." This she does, telling
Mary of her praiseworthy intention: "Order thyself, for no
small contention has arisen concerning thee." That the
author imagines that this is convincing proof to the detractors of this mystery his conclusion shows clearly
enough: "Salome made trial and came out and said: Woe
unto my iniquity and my unbelief, because I have tempted
the living God, and my hand is dried up as by fire, and
falls away from me" (Prot. 20. 1).

The punishment which befalls this incredulous woman
is meant to impress on the reader that he should not doubt
the Omnipotence of God, to whom "nothing is impossible."
As it were to round off this distressing incident, the Lord,
by a final marvel, brings the midwife to belief:

An angel of the Lord appeared to her, saying, Salome,
Salome, the Lord has heard you: bring your hand near to

the young child and take him up. Then Salome took the
child in her arms and said: I will worship him because a
great King is born in Israel. And immediately Salome was
healed and she went out of the cave justified (Prot. 20. 3).

Thus closes the great issue which had arisen on the
subject of virginal childbirth. The two midwives really
personify the partisans and adversaries of the mystery:
Zelomi accepted the issue in simple faith: she represents
those Jews who were converted to the Christian faith from
the beginning. Salome, on the other hand, symbolized
those Israelites who at the time of the writer were hostile
to the Christian faith. Like their fathers, they demanded
signs from heaven, and tangible proof of what they had to
believe. Perhaps the midwife who was first punished for
her unbelief and then, by the grace of God, converted,
would be a stimulus for those holding back.

At all events, it is pseudo-Matthew, in the sixth century, who has drawn the chief lesson from these events of
the virginal birth. He finishes the story by putting these
words on Zelomi's lips: "It has never been heard . . .
that the birth of a son should show his mother a virgin."
That is why we must say of Mary that "a virgin has conceived, a virgin has brought forth, and a virgin she remains" (Ps-Matt. 13. 3).

THE PERPETUAL VIRGINITY OF MARY

"A virgin has conceived; a virgin has brought forth; a
virgin she remains." This phrase expresses perfectly the
belief which the Protevangelium and its successors have
wished to reveal in their popular history of Mary. And it
is a matter of the greatest interest to notice that this is
exactly the faith which the Church has ever taught: the
perpetual virginity of Mary. The Catholic faith holds that

Mary was not only a virgin before her childbirth, but during it, and after it until her death.[4]

The Protevangelium and pseudo-Matthew are then in the full stream of the purest Catholic tradition. In the fourth century the Doctors of the Church, Ambrose and Jerome, showed that her virginity during and after birth were truths of the Catholic Faith. Her virginity before birth was too explicit in Scripture to need to be established.

If belief in Mary's complete and perpetual virginity was not fully established in the first centuries, the reason is that the Church before elucidating the mystery of Mary had to defend the faith in Christ against manifold heresies.[5] But even if it was not in the forefront, faith in the Blessed Virgin was nonetheless alive in the hearts of the faithful. The Protevangelium is a valuable witness to popular belief in the perpetual virginity of Mary. It has not created this belief: rather it has drawn upon the piety of its time and provides evidence for it, haphazard and imperfect, no doubt, but traditional all the same.

If the authority of the Church only pronounced definitively on Mary's perpetual virginity in the seventh century, it was because, as in other fields, an interval of time was necessary to consider the matter carefully. The history of dogma shows that the piety of the faithful forestalls the reflection of the theologians. *Lex orandi, lex credendi*: the law of prayer is the law of faith. It was from the universal instinct of the faithful, carefully tested by Scripture and Tradition, that the Council of the Lateran could define in 649: "if anyone does not acknowledge that the Immaculate and ever Virgin Mary did not conceive the Word of God through the Holy Ghost, without human seed; and

---

[4] The Church uses the following Latin formula: *virginitas ante partum, in partu et post partum.* Cf. *Mary, the Mother of God*, pp. 49-59.

[5] Cf. in this series, *What is the Trinity?* pp. 60 following.

has given birth, while her virginity remained inviolate, even after birth: let him be anathema! (3rd Canon: Denzinger No. 256).

Scripture, we must observe once again, is the basis of this truth of the faith; we have already mentioned the passage of St Matthew where he says of Joseph: "And Joseph awoke from sleep. . . . taking his wife to himself; and he had not known her when she bore a son" (Matt. 1. 24-25).

When we remember that the verb "to know" among the Jews indicated conjugal relations, it will be admitted that this key phrase asserts the virginity of Mary "before" and "in" childbirth. That Joseph had not had intercourse with Mary from their cohabitation till the birth of Jesus, proves that she who conceived by the Holy Spirit gave birth without losing her virginity. If we ask whether Mary remained a virgin, "after" the birth of Jesus and till her death, St Matthew says nothing, because he was not then dealing with events after the birth of Christ.

The critics, especially Protestants, have not failed to make the most of the silence of the evangelists on this latter point. Using arguments already adduced in early times, they have exploited texts which appear to be opposed to the virginity *post partum* of Mary. Did not St Luke call Jesus the "first born" son of Mary? (2. 7). And the synoptics speak of the "brothers" and "sisters" of Jesus.[6]

A deeper understanding of the meaning of these words in the Jewish language has now dispelled these apparent objections. It is accepted today that the title of "first born" was given to the male child who was the heir, without in any way implying the birth of other children. In fact we

---

[6] Cf. Mark 6.3. The people of Nazareth said of Jesus: "Is not this the carpenter, the brother of James and Joseph and Judas and Simon. Do not his sisters live here near us?"

say among ourselves that a woman has just had her first born without deciding whether she will have others. As to the brothers and sisters of Jesus spoken of by the Gospel, these were in all certainty cousins of our Lord. The word "brother" has among the Semites a fairly elastic use. It includes near relatives, cousins or nephews, and even simple neighbours. The Bible is quite convincing on this point. Abraham addressed his nephew Lot: "Let us have no strife between us . . . for we are brethren" (Gen. 13. 9), and Jesus himself speaking of his disciples, said: "Here are my mother and my brethren! If anyone does the will of my Father who is in heaven, he is my brother, and sister, and mother" (Matt. 12. 49-50).

And Scripture is not entirely silent on the subject of Mary's virginity after the birth of Christ. St John relates how she and the beloved disciple stood at the foot of the cross (John 19. 25-7). Before his death Jesus entrusted his mother to the tender care of the disciple with the words: "This is thy mother," and from that time the disciple took her into his "own keeping." This touching scene shows that when her only son was dead Mary had no other support than the most faithful friend of Jesus. If she had had another child besides Jesus would she not have been welcomed by him? And the Gospel records: Mary whose virginity was ever spotless was confided to the virginal Apostle. For we know from the Gospel that St John, like the Baptist, had chosen to remain a virgin: both came from an Essenian background, and shared its spirituality and customs.[7]

[7] These indications are drawn from St. John (1. 35-7); in this passage Jesus meets John the Baptist who was then "with two of his disciples." One was Andrew (v. 40): the other John, who always preserves his anonymity in his own Gospel. It was certainly he who was led to Jesus by the Baptist. We know that the latter, from his life and teaching, had connections with the Essenes, especially on the matter of celibacy.

Tradition and the Magisterium of the Church, which are the authentic interpreters of revelation, founded on the scriptural texts we have mentioned, have firmly maintained Mary's perpetual virginity. This doctrine has grown slowly, but with a certainty which no heresy can undermine.

We conclude by a further glance at these apocryphal writings. As popular links with the origins of Christianity they served at first in their own way as a defence of the data of revelation. Their thesis was perfectly orthodox. But it is obvious that had they given more attention to the restrained narrative of the Gospel they would have avoided much of their luxuriance of imagination. Troubled by the mention of the brothers and sisters of Jesus mentioned in the Gospel, which would seem to put in question Mary's perpetual virginity, they have solved the problem by making them the children not of Mary but of Joseph by a former marriage. Their mother being dead they were now old enough to be present at the birth of Jesus in the cave: if they then became "the brothers and sisters" of Jesus, no one could believe that they were born of Mary.

CHAPTER VII

A DEFENCE OF THE

VIRGIN MOTHER

The preceding chapters can be summed up by saying that the gospels of pseudo-James and the pseudo-Matthew are an ardent defence of the Virgin Mother. They have set out to elucidate this paradox of two words, the Virgin-Mother. To do this they have had one single end in view, to defend by vivid explanations the complete virginity of Mary, even in her motherhood itself.

We can appreciate better at the end of our examination what underlying intentions governed the choice and variety of their narratives. Beneath picturesque and naïve stories these apocryphal writings were attacking the heresies of their time. For already in the first century some were found to deny that Christ had been born of a virgin: this was a dangerous threat to the faith.

THE VALUE OF THE APOCRYPHAL WRITINGS ON MARY

It was not only the Fathers and Doctors of the Church —Justin and Irenaeus in the second century, Ambrose and Augustine in the fourth century—but all the faithful, from the beginning, who repudiated this pernicious error. Those anonymous Christian communities held firmly the they had received from the apostles. The unknown James and Matthew were found, then, to be the popular expression of the faith in the Virgin Mother. We have seen how these authors wished to demonstrate, as graphically as possible, that Mary had received the privilege of being "the Blessed Virgin" who gave the Saviour to the world. Not only had God chosen her from her Mother's womb, as shown by the great miracle of her birth: he had also preserved her from every stain during her youth. Brought up in the Temple in a quasi-monastic routine, the girl had while still very young vowed her virginity to God. She had not been unfaithful to this even when living with Joseph. Lastly, all that surrounded the conception and birth of Jesus prove beyond question that she remained a virgin in her very motherhood.

That pseudo-James and pseudo-Matthew composed their "gospels" to prove this perpetual virginity of Mary, and offered them as "supplements" to the official records, should not greatly surprise us. We have already remarked that the earliest Christian literature tended to imitate the finished forms in which the inspired writers expressed themselves. Our authors only borrowed, then, from their distinguished predecessors the literary form which would give their narratives the greatest chance of convincing and edifying. The biblical type which we have defined as an edifying narrative based on scripture certainly enabled them to explain to people at large the belief in the intact virginity of the Mother of God.

THE DEFECTS OF THIS FORM OF WRITING

Certain abuses seem to have been inseparable from such writings. To imitate scripture is surely to parody it, and the apocryphal writings have not been free from this. Encouraged by popular craving for edifying stories, they have only too readily given free rein to their imagination. The curiosity of the faithful has contributed not a little to encourage them. These are venerable traditions which may well have a foundation in history, but legend has so far taken possession of them as to forbid us even to assign the precise degree of their historical basis. And here an objective comparison of the apocryphal writings with the canonical Gospels presents itself: on the historical level nothing will ever equal the gospel narratives. As we have seen the apocryphal writings allow themselves too great a liberty of expression to be at all trustworthy on all points. The reader can be in no doubt whatever: the narratives of St Luke and St Matthew breathe an air of authenticity: pseudo-James and pseudo-Matthew lead us from an extravagant realism to an altogether otherworldly idealism.

But if there is no danger today of any doubt about the relative value of Scripture and its imitations, it can be said that owing to their early date and perfect orthodoxy of view the apocryphal gospels have powerfully assisted devotion to Mary to flourish in the Church. Among the works which the Christian community early rejected from the list of inspired works[1] these have rightly been greatly respected. In the preface to his critical edition of the Protevangelium Fr Amann states: "The venerable legends that it has put into circulation and which are the basis of almost all the lives of the Blessed Virgin have become incorporated into the ordinary teaching of the Doctors. A theologian today cannot ignore the great place that the Blessed Virgin held in the popular piety of the second century." [2]

This justifies the Church's traditional veneration of our Lady. It is because the Church has found nourishment for

---

[1] We shall speak of this rejection at the end of the book.
[2] E. Amann, *Le Protévangile de Jacques* (Paris, 1910), p. vii.

the life of prayer and an enrichment of her faith in these legends that her liturgy has inscribed in the calendar of feasts of our Lady some of the elements of popular tradition. On August 16th she honours St Joachim; on July 26th, St Anne. She keeps the "Birthday of Mary" on September 8th and the Presentation in the Temple on November 21st. All these feasts have their origins solely in the apocryphal narratives. But the liturgy is not a place for historical research: it is the expression of the Church's faith in Mary in its fullness. Through all these feasts the Church praises the blessed Virgin, the Mother of God, the model of all the saints and of all consecrated souls.

CHAPTER VIII

THE ASSUMPTION OF
THE BLESSED VIRGIN

THE BOOK ON THE "PASSING OF MARY"

When we pass from the Gospel of the Infancy we seem to be leaving our Saviour's Mother behind us. The Synoptics only speak of her once more, and that by chance: once during his public ministry while Jesus was addressing the crowd, he was told that his Mother and his brethren were there and wished to see him (Mark 3. 31-5). We know what follows: he quietly refuses, for the sake of his mission. His real family are those who do the Will of God. This episode is revealing: even the Mother of Jesus must give way to her Son's mission.

The Apostle John is the only one who brings out that this effacement was not due to bodily absence. If Mary stood aside during the public ministry of Jesus, she was present at the beginning and the end. It was she who at Cana gave the signal for the beginning of his redemptive work, by her intervention at his first miracle (John 2. 1-11). And she was intimately associated with the final act on Calvary (John 19. 25).

But are we to believe that her work was finished after this? The inspired writings give no further hint. Except for a verse in the Acts of the Apostles which tells us that the Mother of Jesus on Calvary becoming also "the mother of believers," assumed this rôle and shared in the prayer and life of the infant Church (Acts 1. 13-4). After that the inspired books are quite silent: we know nothing about her final end.

The apocryphal writings have sought to make up for this silence. A multitude of questions disturbed the mind of the Christian: what had become of Mary at her end? How had she passed from this life to the next? Had oral tradition preserved any record of these moments? Several accounts gave an answer to these questions: Mary ascended to heaven like the risen Christ. So arose the stories connected with Mary's Assumption.

Towards the end of the fifth century we find included among apocryphal writings in a list attributed to Pope Gelasius a work entitled *Transitus Sanctae Mariae,* the Passing of Blessed Mary from this world to the next.

This work, written possibly in Greek, has come down to us in about twenty editions, more or less inaccurate. Of the two principal, one Latin, the other Arabic, it is the former which shows the greatest restraint and it is the one to which we shall refer here.

It is a vivid text, full of interest and purports to be the work of Melito, Bishop of Sardis in the second century. In reality it is an anonymous and later text of the fifth century which has carefully eliminated anything in the earlier editions judged to be too credulous. What can be said of its value? In spite of certain historical inaccuracies, this edition is doctrinally sound and is a valuable witness to belief in the Assumption at a relatively early age.

DEATH AND BURIAL OF MARY

In the twenty-second year after Jesus Christ had conquered death and ascended into heaven, Mary, burning with longing for Christ, began to weep one day alone in her own house. . . . [An angel visits her for a second annunciation, that of her own death and assumption to God.]

See, he said, I have brought thee a palm branch[1] from the paradise of God, which thou wilt cause to be carried before thy bier when on the third day thou wilt be taken up from the body. For the Son awaits you with Thrones and Angels and all the Powers of heaven. Then Mary said to the angel: I beg that all the apostles of my Lord Jesus Christ be assembled around me. The angel replied: by the power of Jesus Christ all the apostles will be led here today. (*Trans. Mar.* 3.)

The angel left her, and Mary put on her best garments and went to the Garden of Olives, carrying the Palm. In the very same spot as her Son she made this earnest prayer; that Jesus would not suffer the powers of evil to have dominion over her at her death. Then we are abruptly taken back to the house in Jerusalem, where she is in her agony.

[Suddenly:] by the command of God, all the apostles were snatched up, raised on a cloud from the places where they were preaching the word of God and set down before the door of the house in which Mary dwelt. And saluting each other, they wondered saying: What is the cause for which the Lord has assembled us here? (*Trans. Mar.* 5.)

St John who had received the charge of Mary at the death of Jesus (John 19. 27) was the first to be miraculously transplanted. He brought his fellow apostles to Mary and told them of her approaching death. Mary also confirmed the cause of their sudden reunion: "The Lord has brought you here to console me in the anguish which is coming upon me. I implore you that you watch till the hour in which the Lord comes and I shall depart from the body" (*Trans. Mar.* 6).

In the Gospel Jesus had urged his disciples to watch and pray with him during his agony (Matt. 26. 40-1).

[1] This is the "palm" of the saints, the sign of their abode in paradise.

Three days passed by, "suddenly the Lord came with a great multitude of angels . . ." and speaking to his Mother he said to her "Come, most precious pearl, into the joy of eternal life" (*Trans. Mar.* 7).

Mary then addresses a last petition to her Son to be spared falling into the hands of Satan. And her Son made this beautiful promise to her:

> When . . . I was hanging on the cross, the Prince of Darkness came to me, but as he was able to find in me no trace of his work, he went off vanquished and trodden under foot. But thou shalt see him according to the common law of the human race to which thou conformest in dying. But he will not be able to harm thee, for he has nothing of his own in thee, and I shall be with thee to protect thee. . . .

Nothing can better explain the underlying reason for the events which are to follow—the Blessed Virgin is preserved from the consequences of sin which she has never known: "When the Lord had said this Mary reclined on her bed, and giving thanks to God, gave up her spirit."

And Christ gave his Mother's soul to the archangel Michael, the guardian of Paradise, and directed the Apostles to prepare for the funeral. And certain virgins then took the body to lay it out: the author emphasizes: "When they had taken off her clothes, that sacred body shone with so much brightness that only by the goodness of God could it be touched. It was perfectly pure and in no way contaminated (*Trans. Mar.* 10).

The funeral procession was soon formed. Peter and Paul, "pillars of the Church" carried the coffin; while John the virgin apostle carried "the palm of light." The other apostles joined in the procession, singing the praises of God. The people of Jerusalem followed in the wake of the body. A Jewish priest, who publicly denied both the divinity of Christ and the virginity of Mary, was there and then convinced and miraculously converted.

The apostles laid the body in a new tomb and having closed it they sat down outside as God had commanded. More happy in mind than when Christ came forth living from the grave, they were now to be witnesses of the resurrection and assumption into heaven of Mary.

THE RESURRECTION AND "ASSUMPTION" OF MARY

The Lord came quickly without any delay and surprised the apostles at the tomb. He asked them what special honour he, Jesus, could accord to his Mother in view of her special rôle here below. They all unanimously answered:

Lord, thou hast chosen beforehand this thy servant to becomes a spotless dwelling for thyself . . . it seems to us thy servants to be right, that just as having vanquished death thou reignest in glory, so, raising up again the body of thy Mother, thou shouldest take her with Thee in joy unto heaven (*Trans. Mar.* 16). This is supremely the moment of the "privilege" of the Assumption. The Lord straightway orders the archangel Michael to bring the soul of Mary. And while the apostles were out of themselves, the stone of the tomb was rolled back and the Lord reunites Mary's body to her living soul with the words: "Arise, my beloved, thou who hast not known corruption through intercourse with man shalt not suffer the destruction of the body in the tomb" (*Trans. Mar.* 16).

Mary rises immediately and is embraced by her Son who delivers her to the angels to be conducted to paradise. Mary is then lifted up "body and soul" to heaven by the angels after the Lord.[2] The narrator concludes: "The

[2] We notice that Mary was carried up by the angels. This is to emphasize the difference from Jesus who ascended by his own power. Mary owes her resurrection and "assumption" to the power of her Son: so we speak of the Ascension of Jesus and of the Assumption of Mary to mark the difference.

apostles were taken up in the clouds and returned to the place allotted every one for his preaching, and told the great things of God and praised the Lord Jesus Christ."

MERITS AND DEFECTS OF THE NARRATIVE

A priori it might be thought that the *Transitus Mariae* is an echo of a primitive oral tradition based on genuine historical memories. This kind of writing is the same as the Protevangelium of James and pseudo-Matthew on the life of Mary; it is an *haggadah midrash*. But the haggadah has here taken many more liberties with history since the Gospel gave it no facts at all. Many details included in it are quite gratuitous. For instance, the palm branch which the angel carries as a sign to Mary of her early entry into paradise. The love of the marvellous is shown above all in the extremely unlikely transport of the apostles to Mary's deathbed. But perhaps it is in imitation of Scripture that we are shown Mary united to the apostles before an important event, just as she was before Pentecost. Moreover, the scriptural model of the narrative is clear. The burial of Mary, her return to life and being carried up to heaven are only a free transposition of the Gospel story of Jesus: his burial, and his resurrection followed by the Ascension. Once again, the book of the Passing of Mary is an edifying narrative which has its origins in a scriptural model: it is a *midrash*.

To pass a valid judgement on the merits and demerits of a work of this kind we have to consider the literary character of the work. On the purely historical level its authenticity must be considered very doubtful. When the Gospel spoke of the Pasch of Jesus, that is, his "passage" from this world to his Father, it offered serious guarantees and at the same time respected it as a "mystery." The evangelists absolutely refused to describe miraculous events which were altogether beyond their conception. They offered certain details as proof: the linen cloths and the veil found in the empty tomb (John 20. 6), the various appearances of the risen Christ (Matt. 28. 16-20). The apocryphal writer has no hesitation in describing, as far as he can, the "Passing of Mary" even to the most unlikely details. Consider, for instance, the scene where Christ having descended from heaven, in the presence of the apostles, performs the reuniting of Mary's dead body with her living soul. Such scenes belong rather to the world of the imagination than to reality.

But a narrative is not entirely condemned by its historical inaccuracy: otherwise all narratives of an edifying kind would be valueless. Since the "Passing of Mary" is a description of her last end on the model of the Gospel's description of the passing of Jesus from earth to heaven, we must look beneath the imagery for the idea governing this pious fraud.

And the idea is this: Mary at her death was associated with the glory of her Son. Like him, she finds herself in heaven, body as well as soul. The narrative has quite definite reasons for this corporal glorification of Mary. Mary resembles Jesus perfectly, and through her virginity, preserved intact until death, she was sinless like him. How could her end, then, be different from his? As conqueror of death, her Son had ascended into heaven with the glorified body of his resurrection. Could Mary, who shared with him the privilege of being sinless, experience the corruption of her spotless flesh in the tomb? Logic demanded that she, like Christ, should escape the terrors of death, the consequence of our sinful state.

This is why the author of the "Passing of Mary," as an echo of the belief of his age, has, under this legendary form, put forward sound doctrine. While for obvious reasons it cannot be counted as a "Page of the Gospel," in the line of thought his narrative is nonetheless irreproachable, and conforms exactly to Catholic teaching on Mary's Assumption.

CATHOLIC FAITH IN THE ASSUMPTION

There is one point on which we must be quite clear. The Catholic Faith in the Assumption does not depend in any way on the apocryphal narrative that we have just described. If the date of its appearance—the fifth century—makes the "Passing of Mary" noticeably earlier than the major witnesses of tradition (which appeared in the seventh century), this does not prove that the Church based her belief on a more or less legendary work. In 1950 Pope Pius XII proclaimed as a divinely revealed truth that "Mary, the Immaculate Mother of God, ever Virgin, was at the end of her earthly life, raised to the glory of heaven in body as well as in soul." In doing this Pius XII did not base his pronouncement on a fictitious work of the imagination. He ratified the fundamental datum of Scripture, which a gradual but living and sure tradition has made explicit and finally enjoined on the clear consciousness of the Church.

PART II

LEGENDARY STORIES OF THE INFANCY OF JESUS

INTRODUCTION

ARABIC AND ARMENIAN GOSPELS OF THE INFANCY

Hitherto the apocryphal writings that we have encountered have not been concerned with Christ, but with Mary. No doubt the Protevangelium and pseudo-Matthew were concerned with the birth of Jesus, but when that came to pass their work as a preface to the inspired Gospel of the Infancy was done. The works which we now consider deal with this infancy.

A "Narrative of the Infancy of the Lord by Thomas the Israelite, the Philosopher" towards the fifth century had combined together various short stories and legends hitherto independent. The mystery of this fusion has never been cleared up, but it is thought that this work, at first combined with the Protevangelium of pseudo-James, was considerably amplified on its diffusion among the Arabs, Armenians and Persians. There resulted from this a continuous narrative of the infancy of Christ, and this we have in two different forms: the Arabic gospel and the Armenian gospel of the Infancy. The Arabic gospel owes its name to the repute that it long had in Arabia. It dates from the sixth century. It follows the course of the Gospel narrative on the flight into Egypt and the hidden life.

Its companion the Armenian gospel of the Infancy is later. Especially popular among the Persians, it develops the wondrous story of the Magi, who according to it, came from that country.

These two verbose collections of stories of the Infancy of Christ have this in common: their childish love of the marvellous which makes one think of the stories in the *Thousand and One Nights*. In this atmosphere the *haggadah* absolves itself of all historical scruples: it soars aloft, with at times a brazen lack of constraint.

It is true enough that the Infancy of Christ lends itself— nothing more so—to legend. Two short chapters of Luke and two of Matthew is all that the Gospel offers us on the early youth of the Saviour. Are we, then, without any information about the deeds and words of the Child in the bosom of the holy family? The two Evangelists only report the public and major events which stand out in the childhood of Jesus. Their information is comprised under four heads: the visit of the Magi and the flight into Egypt, according to St Matthew (2. 1-18); the presentation of Jesus in the Temple and the discovery of him among the Doctors at the age of twelve, according to St Luke (2. 22-50). Apart from these episodes, the inspired Gospel accepts the mystery of the "hidden life" at Nazareth which constitutes so to say the background of the picture.

The early generations were intrigued by this reticence and eagerly sought to lift the veil which covered our Saviour's early years: this was the work of the apocryphal writings, showing sometimes a touching devotion, at others an excess of curiosity which passes from the grotesque to the trivial.

CHAPTER IX

CHILDHOOD OF JESUS

THE STABLE, THE OX AND THE ASS

There are traditions whose origins are unknown to us. This is true of the crib at Christmas. In order to offer a better occasion for the appreciation of its charm the delightful passage by which the Protevangelium introduces the story of the Nativity was not quoted earlier in the book:

> And they (Joseph and Mary) came to the middle of the journey, and Mary said to him: Take me down from the ass, for that which is within me presses me to come forth. And he took her down from the ass and said: Where shall I take thee to hide thy shame, for the place is desert. And he found a cave there and brought her into it. (Prot. 17. 3-18. 1).

We notice that the Protevangelium puts the place of the birth outside Bethlehem and in the middle of the journey. If we look at a map, we see that between Jerusalem and Bethlehem the only serviceable road was that of the desert of Juda, along the edge of the Dead Sea. We know that in this desert, in the rocky cliffs which dominate the valley of the Jordan, there have recently been discovered the famous caves in which the Essenian monks lived. Without doubt the author considered that Jesus was born in one of these natural desert caves.

St Luke will have none of this, as his narrative makes plain. The birth occurred in the actual town of Bethlehem, which was the ancestral town of David, of whom Jesus was the messianic anti-type. The Evangelist does not say that the birth happened in a cave but in a "manger," which no doubt belonged to a house in which the poor, refused admittance to the inns, collected. Let us read the passage again:

> Joseph . . . came up from the town of Nazareth, in Galilee, to David's city in Judaea, the city called Bethlehem . . . and it was while they were still there that the time came for her delivery. She brought forth a son, her firstborn, whom she wrapped in his swaddling clothes, and laid in a manger, because there was no room for them in the inn. (Luke 2. 4-7).

The word "manger" from which animals eat shows us that we are in a stable. A town like Bethlehem would not be without them. The raising of cattle was the chief occupation in this district. The presence of shepherds in the district and the fact that they were first warned of the event by the angels, is a sufficient indication of this.

Thus in the Protevangelium in the second century the stable of Bethlehem has been transformed into a desert cave. The detail is important, because since then our cribs have traditionally adopted the form of rocky caves. It is true that apart from the Gospel an ancient and solid tradition has located the birth of Christ in a cave near Bethlehem. As early as 150 St Justin says "as Joseph could find no lodging in the village, he settled in a nearby cave." And in the third century Origen mentions that it was the practice to show this cave "out in the country" to pilgrims. It was on this spot that in 325 the Emperor Constantine built the Basilica of the Nativity.

Must we then choose between the stable and the cave? There is no need. In Palestine, even today, caves dug in the hillside serve both as stables for animals and dwellings for the poor. In the time of our Lord, Bethlehem probably offered such shelter to those who could get nothing else, and in one of these Mary would have taken shelter when her delivery came upon her.

But it gave the Protevangelium an opportunity of illustrating the verse of Isaias which in the Greek version of the Bible says of the Messiah that he will dwell in "a cave hewn out of rock" (cf. Isaias 33. 16).

Scripture offered many other sources on which to draw. The ingenious discoveries of the apocryphal writings were not confined to the setting of the Nativity, but included the characters too. It is the apocryphal gospels which have brought to the Divine Infant the two animals now always found in our cribs, the ox and the ass. The Protevangelium says nothing about these animals. But his successor, pseudo-Matthew in the sixth century, puts both of them round the Infant, as the first of his devout worshippers. We read: "Mary put the babe in the manger[1] and the ox and ass adored him." Further on: "these animals worshipped unceasingly the babe between them" (Ps-Matt. 14. 1).

So we are well informed of the part which the animal characters play in our cribs. Are we to insist in asking whence pseudo-Matthew obtained the touching idea of the "worship" of Jesus by these animals? He himself explains: "And thus was fulfilled what the prophet Isaias had foretold: ox recognizes its owner, ass knows the way to its master's crib" (Isaias 1. 3). He also quotes from Habakuk: "Thou shalt reveal thyself in the midst of two animals" (Hab. 3. 2, Greek).

It is obvious that in the literal sense these verses had a poetic and not a strictly prophetic value. We can see what has happened. Not content with basing himself on the

---

[1] This apocryphal writer has harmonized the data of the Gospel and Tradition. While he puts the birth of Christ in a cave, he states that three days afterwards the new born babe was brought back into a stable among the animals.

Gospel narrative of the Nativity, the author has sought out in Scripture whatever, in its literal meaning, might serve his purpose. One or two scriptural references sufficed to turn poetic quotations into historical facts. Once more we encounter the rule of the *midrash*.

THE MAGI AS THREE KINGS

Each year the Epiphany brings us to the "manifestation" of the Son of God to the pagan world. This feast commemorates the coming of the Magi, those strangers from afar, to the crib. But how do we know that the Magi were kings? And, an even more interesting detail, how is it that these famous men are three in number and answer to the delightful names of Gaspar, Melchior and Balthazar?

We have to acknowledge that the Gospel has said not a single word about all this. St Matthew, who mentions the visit of the wise men, says nothing of their being rich, or learned or of royal dignity; nor does he even mention their number. If he had known their names, no doubt he would have told us. But this is all he has to say: "Jesus was born at Bethlehem, in Juda, in the days of King Herod. And thereupon certain wise men came out of the east to Jerusalem" (Matt. 2. 1). Unquestionably for the evangelist and his contemporaries the term Magi simply meant those learned in astrology, which was then the great science of the oriental world. Whence did they come? The East— a studiously vague term, for the East in Palestine is the Arabian desert on the eastern side of the Jordan.

In short, the Gospel shows considerable reserve on the subject, and offers nothing to satisfy our curiosity. So the apocryphal writings have sought to quench the popular thirst for detail.

It must be admitted that the Arabic Gospel and its like had some right to claim to supply information on this point, since they originated in the remote regions from which the Magi were said to have come. And an old Arabian text was the first to give information on the subject. According to this, Zoroaster, the founder of Magism in the sixth century before Christ, had prophesied the epoque which should lead his descendants to the crib. This legend was the starting point of the narratives that we are now to read.

The Armenian Gospel of the Infancy tells us that at the time foretold by the ancestor of the Magi, an angel of God was sent in haste to the land of the Persians to announce to them the birth of the King of the Jews. It was then that the famous description was given: "Three brothers were the Kings of the Magi: the first, Melchon,[2] reigned over the Persians: the second, Balthazar, reigned over the Indians: the third, Gasper, possessed the land of the Arabians."

Enamoured of astrology, in their study of the sky these three oriental sovereigns had seen a star more brilliant than the others. As they more or less identified their gods with the stars, they concluded from this phenomenon that a god had just been born whose reign should eclipse all the sovereigns of the earth.[3] And so began the journey by the star. Immediately abandoning the worship of their inferior deities, the three Magi followed the bright star to the place where lay the crying King of Kings and incarnate God of Gods. As in Gospel, they offered him their princely gifts. A Syriac manuscript tells us that in return, in order that royal protocol should not be violated, they received from the Saviour this priceless gift: "Mary took one of Jesus' swaddling clothes and gave it to them. They received it from her hands with faith, as a priceless gift."

[2] Afterwards corrupted into Melchior.
[3] In the East the king was the incarnation of a divinity or his earthly lieutenant.

After they had offered their homage the miraculous star led them back to their own land. The whole of Persia rejoiced at their return, while they, who were now converted to the true God, set about the conversion of their subjects, still idolaters. The precious swaddling band of the Infant Jesus powerfully seconded their discourses: it was thrown into a huge fire, the flames of which were being adored by the people; at first it turned red in the flames and was thought to be burning; then the fire died down and it was drawn from the ashes whiter and more substantial than before. Such a miracle was startling. Its witnesses came forward to venerate such a relic of Christ saying: "This must be, without any doubt, the garment of the God of gods, since the divine fire could not burn it."

They believed in Jesus. And so finished the strange adventure of the three Kings who among their own people became the first Christian missionaries.

The Armenian Gospel of the Infancy, has, obviously, only elaborated the narrative of St Matthew. The word picture which he paints—with an abundance of local colour —carries on the lesson only suggested by the Gospel. The Epiphany by its very name is the manifestation of the divinity of Christ to the gentiles. To bring out the significance of the adoration of the Magi, and especially through their action, the coming of the people which they represent to the faith, it was enough for the author to base his pious narrative on a few selected passages of Scripture.

The rising of a miraculous star was expected in the East as the sign of the birth of the Messiah. Balaam, the soothsayer of Arabia, had foretold of the King of the Jews: "I see a star that rises out of Jacob, a stem that springs from Israel's root" (Numbers 24. 17).

A magnificent text of Isaias—the messianic prophet— had clearly foretold that the wise men from the East would be kings, coming from a distant country to worship the true God and to believe in him with all their people: "Rise up, Jerusalem, and shine forth; thy dawn has come, breaks the glory of the Lord upon thee! . . . those rays of thine shall light the Gentiles on their path; Kings shall walk in the splendour of thy sunrise . . . bringing all the men of Saba[4] with their gifts of gold and incense, their cry of praise to the Lord" (Isaias 60. 1-6).

The outburst of poetic imagery has not led the Gospel into any excess of words or imagination. The sacred narrative of the Magi is only a restrained meditation on this profound truth: in the Infant of Bethlehem it is God in person who has manifested himself to the world. Henceforth all the nations of the earth ought to recognize the King of heaven and enter into his Kingdom. But the apocryphal writers have presented this message in a vivid form to a people avid for a story.

LIGHT ON THE HIDDEN LIFE

The hidden life of Jesus begins with the hasty flight of the Holy Family into Egypt. In a few lines St Matthew describes this first escape of the Child, far away from all worldly agitation. With its normal reticence the Gospel has not described either the exact place in which Jesus was hidden from the anger of Herod the false "King of the Jews":[5] nor the vicissitudes of that cruel journey.

Both history and geography absolve us from having to picture a long journey through the desert to the Nile delta. At that time, as today, the frontier between Israel and Egypt passed through the desert of Negeb to the south of

---

[4] The Kingdom of Arabia, celebrated already when the Queen of Saba came to Solomon with her gifts and recognized in him a type of the Messiah (3 Kings 10. 6-7).

[5] This ruler, who was not a Jew, had usurped the throne of Juda with the support of the Romans. He greatly feared for his title and his crown.

Juda. This frontier, quite near to Bethlehem, was a highway for the frequent trade caravans and a refuge zone for the crowd of emigrants from both countries. It was here, no doubt, that the Child and his parents awaited the tyrant's death before returning to their country.[6]

But the apocryphal writers have filled in the historical gaps and the silence of the Gospels, and have changed a cruel flight into a triumphal progress. Instead of submitting in all human weakness to this inexorable destiny, the Child Jesus advances into Egypt as God victorious. He is made to carry through a fantastic epic—in inverse order— just as of old Yahweh led the Hebrews through this heathen land. Now it is God who reveals himself as the master of Egypt. The victorious Exodus is renewed: the Arabic gospel tells us of a temple in an Egyptian city in which the idols fell to pieces at Jesus' feet. Although he was only two years old, the people of Pharaoh recognized him: "There is a hidden and mysterious God. . . . He is the true God. . . . His son's feet have trodden on the soil of Egypt" (Ev. Ar. 10. 2, Syriac version).

This revelation of the true God seems to fulfil a prophecy of Isaias: "See where the Lord comes into Egypt, with the cloud drift for his chariot, and all the false gods of Egypt tremble, the very heart of Egypt melts away (Isaias 19. 1).

According to the Gospel, Christ when he returned from exile began a strictly hidden life. We know no more than that Joseph set up his home not in Juda where Herod's son reigned, but in Galilee, at Nazareth, the small home town of Mary (Matt. 2. 23; Luke 2. 39). We learn nothing of the day to day existence of the Holy Family in this quiet village until Jesus was twelve years old.

The more silent the Gospel, the more intrigued were

---

[6] According to Flavius Josephus, Herod was a sadistic murderer who ended his life by a wholesale slaughter (Ant. Jew. XVII. 181).

the apocryphal writers by the mystery of Nazareth. And since their source was now silent the Arabian and Armenian Gospels did not scruple in giving rein to their love of the miraculous.

CHARMING STORIES

There is in the Arabic Gospel more than one charming story that is almost like a little fairy story. The following is the most pleasing.

When he was seven years old, Jesus was playing with others of his age. The Child and his little friends were playing, making models in clay. Donkeys, cows, birds— each one was boasting of what his imaginative power had succeeded in making. But Jesus, the Creator, suddenly made living beings come from his hands: sparrows flew from between his fingers, and returned quietly to settle on them. In amazement his friends told their parents, who would not believe them. After this, their well behaved children no longer went to play with this budding magician, capable of anything.

On another occasion, Mary sent her son to draw water at the well—a familiar sight in Palestine, both then and now. But the Child filled his pitcher too full, it was too heavy for his little shoulders, and it fell and broke. But never mind. Jesus gathers up the spilt water in a cloak and brings it to his Mother. Mary was full of admiration, and the Arabic Gospel tells, in imitation of St Luke's words: "she kept secretly in her heart all that she saw" (Ev. Ar. 45).

It is obvious enough that such childishness could hardly find a place in the canonical Gospel of the Infancy.

SOME STRANGE ADVENTURES

To say the least, certain of the stories are grotesque. The fancifulness employed borders on the ridiculous and offends good taste.

In the Arabic Gospel there is the curious story of a marriageable young man over whom jealous sorceresses quarrelled. In the end no one was to have him as a husband; they laid a spell on him and the poor man was changed into a mule. His whole family was disconsolate by this metamorphosis; they had to have an animal to live with them. All the wise men and magicians they consulted could not lift the spell. Then the Holy Family passed by. Understanding the unique dignity of the Mother and her Son, the relatives addressed this petition to Mary:

> O Lady Mary have pity on your handmaidens . . . this mule thou seest is our brother, and he has been reduced to this state by the witchcraft of certain women. We beseech thee to have pity on us.
> [Mary was touched by their misfortune, and immediately she] the Lady Mary took up the Lord Jesus and put him on the mule's back. She wept and so did the three women. Then she said to her son, Jesus Christ: My Son, cure this mule by thy almighty power and make him return to a man endowed with reason as he was before. And at the moment that our Lady Mary spoke these words the mule changed his form and became a young man, free from every defect (Ev. Ar. XXI, 2 and 3).

There is something rather shocking in this miracle: we do not like to see the saving actions of Jesus mixed up with such vulgar superstitions. But even so, the story has its interest: it is evidence of Christian faith in the first ages in the intercessory power of Mary. The petition is made reverently and devoutly to "our Lady the Virgin Mary" as if she wielded a special power. And, indeed, it is evident that while Jesus worked the miracle, it was at the intervention of Mary. Scripture shows us instances of this. At the marriage of Cana (John 2. 1-11) Mary interceded with her Son that the wine should not be wanting. There is nothing then that is unorthodox in this episode of the young man changed into a mule: but it is distressing that such undoubted devotion should be expressed in a story of such dubious taste.

SOME UNSEEMLY INCIDENTS

Besides these touching little stories and strange adventures there is also a selection of tales altogether beyond the bounds of common sense, in which the Child Jesus becomes the hero of ridiculous and shabby pranks. His supernatural power is changed into spiteful sorcery, and the Saviour becomes nothing more than a mere magician. The following tale bears this out.

In a scene of childish insolence the Arabic Gospel parodies the Parable of the Good Shepherd. One day when some children of his own age refused to play with him Jesus determined to be revenged upon them. The naughty children hid themselves in an oven as he approached; he asked a group of women where they had hidden themselves. But the women did not know. Then, like a real soothsayer, with a view to revealing the youngsters hidden in the oven, he inquired: "And who are those over there?" As a joke the women answered: "They are three year old goats."

They did not realize how truly they spoke, for Jesus taking them at their word made the boys come out magically changed into goats. He called them and played with them like a mock shepherd. In terror the women protested: "The good shepherd has not come to destroy, but to heal" (Ev. Ar. 40. 1 and 2).

Then, as if he realized that he was not acting quite in accordance with the Gospel the Child restores their human life to his young companions. A disconcerting picture, the reverse of the Good Shepherd, who knows his sheep and loves them.

There are numerous other stories which cheapen both the supernatural power of God, and the life of his creatures. In them Jesus reveals a blind and brutal strength which has no respect for the dignity of creation. Thus in a game the Child begins to ill-treat his companions: in order to win he makes one deaf and the other blind. We encounter even worse examples: "One day as the Lord Jesus was returning home with Joseph, he met a boy who ran up against him and knocked him down. And the Lord Jesus said to him: as you have knocked me down, so shall you fall and not rise again. And at that very moment, the boy fell down and died" (Ev. Ar. 48).

Can this really be considered edifying? It lacks the restraint and dignity of the Gospel. Where is the manifestation on earth of "the kindness of God, our Saviour" (Titus 3. 4). Such a Saviour is neither divine nor human. The apocryphal books would never have retailed such miserable stories about Jesus if they had kept to what St Luke says of the mystery of the Infancy: "And so Jesus advanced in wisdom with the years, and in favour both with God and with men" (Luke 2. 52).

CHAPTER X

THE YOUTH OF JESUS

We can now understand better how eager the apocryphal gospels were to reveal to the world the divinity of Jesus. It was to this end that they accumulated so many marvels round his childhood. Endowed from birth with the overwhelming power of the true God over idols, the Child subsequently showed himself more expert in magic than his companions: it remained to demonstrate that as a young man he possessed wisdom that could confound even the most learned.

JESUS AMONG THE DOCTORS

As in everything else the inspired Gospel preserves a discretion which rings true on the matter of Jesus' knowledge. When St Luke relates the episode of the finding of the Child in the Temple among the doctors (Luke 2. 41-50) it is not to show off his learning. The Child has entered his twelfth year and so is an adolescent. Accompanying his parents on the Passover pilgrimage to Jerusalem he went by himself to the Temple. This escape was deliberate, though Joseph and Mary thought that he was lost. After hunting everywhere, his parents found him: "sitting in the Temple, in the midst of those who taught there" (Luke 2. 46).

These doctors were the religious teachers of the time: learned students of the scriptures, they publicly taught the

Law of Moses. The learning of these "masters," the Rabbis,[1] was greatly respected by the people. If Jesus put himself one day among their audience it was not because he wished to teach them through his divine knowledge. The sacred text in no wise says that he began to teach. An eager pupil, pensive and much advanced for his age he was "listening to them and asking them questions; and all those that heard him were in amazement at his quick understanding and at the answers he gave" (Luke 2. 46-47).

His behaviour was sufficient to make those present realize that he was not just an ordinary boy like others: in him was hidden a higher wisdom. But these masters could not perceive that he was the Son of God in person. The time had not yet come for him to reveal this openly. Thus at the close of this episode he simply emphasizes the mysterious filial relation which unites him to God, his Father: "Could you not tell that I must needs be in the place which belongs to my Father?" (Luke 2. 49).

Undoubtedly Jesus himself is quite aware of his divine Sonship, since he calls God his "Father." But this mystery is still quite unknown to the doctors, since the evangelist said even of his parents, Joseph and Mary that: "These words which he spoke to them were beyond their understanding" (Luke 2. 50).

What a truly human story this is! The inspired Gospel of the Infancy shows us an historical Christ, submitting to all the laws of human existence in his work of revelation.

Swept along in the current of marvellous events which they have verbally created, the apocryphal writers have turned the Gospel narrative all upside down. They give another picture of Jesus sitting among the doctors: the Child, a prodigy of wisdom, sits among the rabbis. It is he who teaches them while they listen dumbfounded. From

---

[1] The name Rabbi is still given to the Jewish masters who teach in the synagogues.

childish lips an all-embracing wisdom answers their questions. Here is the dialogue from the Arabic Gospel between Jesus and the wisest man among his audience, a philospher physician:

> There was one very skilled in natural science, and he asked the Lord Jesus whether he had studied medicine. And he, in reply, explained to him physics and metaphysics . . . the powers and humours of the body: also the number of members and bones, of veins, arteries and nerves; also the effect of heat and dryness, of cold and moisture; what was the operation of the soul upon the body, and its perceptions and powers . . . and other things beyond the created intellect (Ev. Ar. 48. 4).

A good exposition of the medical and philosophical knowledge of the age, which leads the learned man to exclaim: "Lord, from this time, I will be thy disciple and slave!"

And if we ask how the Infant Jesus came by this stupendous range of human learning, the Arabic Gospel tells us that he did not owe it to any human master. At the school to which Joseph and Mary had sent him, he was unwilling to learn the alphabet. It was the master, an eminent Rabbi of Jerusalem, who learnt from the Child: "many other things he began to recount and elucidate which the master himself had never heard or read in any book" (Ev. Ar. 48. 2).

The little prodigy was taken back to his parents, and the master explained: "You have brought me a boy more learned than all the masters. This son of thine has no need of instruction" (Ev. Ar. 48. 3).

A CATECHISM LESSON

It is strange that according to the Arabic Gospel Jesus had only revealed his secular learning to the doctors. St Luke, with much more likelihood, gives us the opposite impression. It was of God, his Father, that he spoke to them, as they were accustomed with the law of Moses.

It was necessary, therefore, to show that the Child had a religious knowledge superior to that of other mortals. The Armenian Gospel has a curious episode which shows Jesus revealing in advance the mystery of the Man-God. Two soldiers meet the Babe and ask who he is. The answer —an excellent theological discourse, explains a string of questions on the mystery of the Incarnation. A soldier asks Jesus: "Are your father and mother alive?"

"Yes, my Father is alive, and indeed is immortal."

"How immortal?"

"Immortal from the beginning, he lives now, and death has no power over him."

Surprised, the soldier presses his enquiry further on this exceptional power: "Who can see him?"

"No one . . . You cannot see him, nor even represent him to yourself."

"Where is he then?"

"In heaven, above this earth."

The questions here become more intimate on the relations uniting Father and Son.

"How can you go to him?"

"I have been and still am with him."

"I don't understand what you say."

Jesus answers that his life with and in the Father is "inexplicable and ineffable" (See John 17. 21). Even so the soldier still presses the matter: "How were you born?"

"My first birth came from the Father, before time: the second occurred on earth."

A human being has never been born twice, on earth and in heaven. The soldier inquires: "How many fathers and how many mothers have you?"

However much the Sibylline answer may seem a quaint pun it is a perfectly accurate expression of the Incarnation: "I have One only Father and no mother: I have a Mother and with her no father."

One might imagine that the questioner would be disconcerted by now. Not at all! He has understood the point. On the one hand Jesus is the Son of God who has begotten him in heaven completely by himself; Jesus is also a man, and derives his human life from a woman. But this woman is a virgin who has had no relation with Joseph, who is therefore not his father.

"If your Father has not seen your mother, how has she conceived you in her womb?"

"Through the operation of a simple word and without the intercourse of any man" [2] (Ev. Ar. 38. 1-4).

So we end this excellent catechism lesson for adults given in such easy fashion by the child. Fundamentally, it is doctrinally quite sound. It explains the knowledge that Jesus certainly had of his divine Sonship, when at twelve years of age he declared to Joseph his foster father that he had a Father in heaven, God (Luke 2. 49).

An omniscient youth, who reveals his knowledge with disconcerting ease: such is the portrait which the apocryphal writings present of the Infant God. But that is not the picture of Christ which the inspired Gospel gives us. As we have said, Jesus scarcely admits to his intimates that he is the Son of God. But certainly at no time does he show off his knowledge of the natural sciences. But this does not mean that Jesus was ignorant of these things. For though he had the knowledge of the greatest savant of his age and our own, the fact remains that Christ had come on earth only to teach "the religion of the Father" and not the secrets of nature. But it is legitimate to ask if

[2] This answer shows that the Armenian Gospel of the Infancy held that the conception took place immediately "the word of the angel" was announced to Mary. In addition there is an allusion to Mary's vow of virginity.

divine Infant, by reason of his divine nature, did not know everything, human as well as divine. Theologians of all time have devoted themselves to this problem of the knowledge of Christ. St Thomas Aquinas has given the surest solution of the problem. For him, there can be no doubt that, given the excellence of his human nature, united to the Divine, Christ must possess all the perfections of human nature and hence the knowledge of all things seen in God.

But to what degree can the Son of God communicate this universal knowledge to men? Here lies the crux of the problem. What Christ saw of God in the depths of his soul, united immediately to God the Word, was strictly incommunicable. Just as the mystics, lifted out of themselves for a moment in ecstasy, cannot express the ineffable content of their vision in words, so Christ, whose soul was ever enlightened by this "beatific vision" of the Father, could not express this intimate and profound experience.

How, then, could he fulfil his mission of the Revealer of God? After St Thomas, theologians teach that Christ possessed "infused" knowledge (because it was given from on high) to know and reveal God's plan for man, the destiny of man and of each individual. All that concerned the salvation of the world Jesus knew and could communicate.

But, as a final requirement of the mystery of the Incarnation, it seems fitting that this knowledge proper to the Revealer of God could only be exercised through the acquired and experimental knowledge common to all men. His function as the Revealer and his consciousness of being the Son of God did not remove Christ from the laws of human existence, and the gradual progression of its growth. Jesus had to learn to read and write, to acquire the learning of his time, and to do this in order, within the limits of his time, to communicate to his contemporaries, in suitable language, what was given him to reveal of God and his designs.

The apocryphal writings are wrong, then, making the Infant Christ speak without paying any attention to the limits which he placed on himself by the very fact of the Incarnation.

CHAPTER XI

THE ABSURDITIES OF
THE INFANCY GOSPELS

St Jerome, an authority on the subject of true and false
scriptures, has given a definitive judgement on these latter.
He speaks of the folly of the apocryphal writings, and we
think that this folly is most evident in these legendary
stories of the infancy of Jesus. And none deserves the
condemnation more than the Arabic and Armenian gospels. Their method can be resumed under two heads: a
lack of respect for the mystery of the Incarnation, and a
confusion between the supernatural and the wondrous.

THE REJECTION OF THE HOUR OF JESUS

The first criticism of the apocryphal writings of the infancy is their lack of respect for the Incarnation. If God
has entered into time and has willed to accept our human
state, it is to adapt his revelation to the rhythm of human
development. Anyone opening the Gospel is struck by this
submission of the Man-God to the law of human growth.
It is only when he has reached the age of thirty that Jesus
begins to proclaim his message and reveal his divinity. A
long retreat preceded this moment. As a child and even
as a young man he had worked no miracle. Let there be
no mistake here: St John tells us quite plainly that Jesus

did his "first miracle" at the marriage feast of Cana, when he began his public life. And it was only gradually that Christ revealed himself as the "Son of God" to the crowds and even his disciples. He said himself that this final revelation had its proper time, kept secret by the Father, which would come when he willed. This "Hour" of Jesus was in no sense anticipated: it was on the Cross and in the glory which followed it, that Jesus realized it. For it was in these events alone that his Divinity was supremely revealed.

The apocryphal writers have rejected this "Hour" of Jesus. Their one idea is to reveal our Saviour's divine omnipotence in his childhood. Hence the unlimited accumulation of wonders and sensational revelations during the hidden life. They were impatient to show to everyone that the Child was God, however difficult it might be to believe. But this apologetical method, based it seems on the highest motive, destroys the very mystery of the Incarnation. If the Jesus of the apocryphal writers seems to be endowed with the Omnipotence of God, he appears as no longer completely human: he is a puppet which a divine hand works from behind the celestial wings.

The divine Child is totally different in reality. The Word made flesh voluntarily submitted to the normal stages of human growth: he did not live as one outside the stream of time, but in accepting our life adapted himself to the teaching of revelation as men can understand it.

THE SUPERNATURAL AND THE MARVELLOUS

The second departure from veracity of these infancy legends lies in the rank confusion of the supernatural with the wondrous.

In the apocryphal narratives the miracles of Jesus are at once ostentatious, useless and misplaced. The Child needlessly multiplies his miracles for spectacular purposes. No doubt they were induced by the naïve curiosity of a people always moved by superhuman adventures. But how can we forgive the authors for depicting all the mischievous tricks of a street urchin, the spiteful and thoroughly reprehensible actions which they ascribe to him? The degredation of what is holy is here a sign of an utterly erroneous idea of the miraculous. In the inspired Gospel Jesus is certainly not a worker of wonders just to startle the crowds. He refused that rôle from the start. We have only to remember the temptation in the desert. Satan endeavoured to induce "the Son of God" to perform startling actions and resounding miracles. Had he not the power to change the stones into bread at once, and to throw himself down from a height without injury? Jesus rejected this ostentatious way of proving his divinity; he says to the devil: "Thou shalt not put the Lord thy God to the proof" (Matt. 4. 7), meaning, "you shall not compel me to perform showy but useless miracles."

When asked for "signs" of his divinity and his redemptive mission Jesus gave them the quality of supernatural and redemptive acts marked by depth and truth. Need we repeat that the miracles of Christ had not only an apologetical end; they were acts which entered into the very scheme of the redemption. Jesus healed the sick, delivered the possessed, raised the dead, because he was Lord of the devil, of sin and of death. All these miracles had as their purpose the deliverance of mankind subject to evil, and the restoration of divine life. In this connection it should be noticed that with each of the physical benefits that he granted, our Saviour demanded an act of faith in his Person and in his saving mission. The forgiveness of sins and purification of the soul are the ultimate purpose of his divine working of miracles.

Definitely, then, there is nothing in common between the exaggerated and fantastic atmosphere of the marvellous which encumbers the legendary infancy of Jesus, and the redemptive work of Jesus "who went about doing good" in a world suffering from a threefold sickness of sin, suffering and death. Gravity is the hall mark of the supernatural.

PART III

THE PUBLIC LIFE OF CHRIST

CHAPTER XII

UNRECORDED WORDS

OF JESUS

FROM THE SPOKEN WORD
TO THE SCRIPTURES

The evangelists who have recorded his message state boldly: it is God himself who speaks in Jesus. Christ was more than a prophet: he was the "Word of God" who became incarnate (John 1. 14) to reveal to the world truth and life. The apostles and the Jewish people both realized that "nobody has ever spoken as this man speaks" (John 7. 46) and again "and they were amazed by his teaching" (Mark 1. 22).

It is necessary to recall here that Jesus himself did not write a single line. Not a word from his pen has been left to us, nor did he ever direct his apostles to write down his message. Like Christ, and as his continuation, their work was to proclaim publicly the "Gospel," the good news of salvation. "Go out all over the world and preach the gospel to the whole of creation" (Mark 16. 15). Again "the Holy Spirit will come upon you, and you will receive strength from him; you are to be my witnesses in Jerusalem . . . and to the ends of the earth" (Acts 1. 8).

Strong in the Spirit they had received at Pentecost (Acts 2. 1-4) and living by the Word which "can penetrate deeper than any two-edged sword" (Hebr. 4. 12), the apostles began to evangelize. But oral preaching of the Gospel soon became insufficient to spread the faith. Groups of believers in Jesus arose here and there, not only in the Holy Land, but in Asia and as far as the West: in the very heart of the Roman empire which then comprised the known world. This rapid extension gave rise to more than one problem. On the one hand the apostles and their assistants were too few in number, and journeys in that age were long and dangerous. Then also, with the passing of time, the voices of those who had been actual witnesses and the first disciples, would cease.

St Paul was the first to commit his preaching to writing. To every place where he had founded a Church he sent "doctrinal letters" to supplement his oral teaching. The first inspired writings were born, then, of circumstances. The publication of St Paul's Epistles between 50 and 65 did not in any way prevent the other apostles from continuing their oral teaching. But the Spirit inspired these also who had known Christ and knew his doctrine to put their witness down in writing before they died. To do this they had no need of scholarship: they committed their memories to writing in the bosom of the infant Church to supply its vital needs.

Collections of the words and deeds of Jesus were already being circulated in the Churches. The early Christians loved to draw upon these for reading and meditating upon the Saviour's life during the time of the public prayer. The apostles and their immediate disciples placed the seal of their personal experience on this living material, hitherto confined within the life of these communities. They composed "the Gospels."

The apostles who had lived in the company of Christ, received his teaching, and had been chosen by him to carry his message to the ends of the earth, authenticated with their apostolical witness what tradition had to tell of Jesus.

Thus the composition of the four Gospels of Mark, Luke, Matthew and John closed the period when Christ's message was given only orally. From now on this message had passed into the "memories of the apostles." They might pass away, but the Church, before the end of the first century[1] was in possession of the precious deposit of Revelation. Of course, oral Tradition was to remain to complement Scripture, of which it is the source, but it could no longer claim to contain any essential truth not contained in the inspired books.

We shall show in due course how, from the second century, the infant Church, the inheritor of the Word of Christ, was clearly aware that the Gospels constituted the "Testament of Jesus," guaranteed by the apostles, to which nothing can be added.

THE LIVING VOICE OF TRADITION

Because the oral preaching of Christ and his disciples preceded the composition of the Gospels, it is not without interest to dwell a little on this initial period when the living Word was still heard. For the oral proclamation of the Gospel still went on even as the Scriptures were taking shape. There is no doubt that for the first Christians oral Tradition was in no sense confined by the literary compilation. The heads of the communities, appointed by the apostles, retained living recollections of their speech. In short, there were two parallel modes of teaching: there was the basic and essential teaching contained in the "memories of the apostles;" this was the primary message which the Holy Spirit had inspired as a guarantee of its authenticity. Then there was the wider oral teaching of the apostles' successors. These latter—bishops or elders— were the link with the age of the spoken message, so that

[1] The New Testament writings were composed between 50-100.

their official teaching could have preserved, side by side with the Gospels, certain historical sayings of Jesus.

There is conclusive evidence that all the *Logia* of Christ —this Greek word is used for the sayings of Jesus—were not preserved in the Gospels. At the end of his Gospel St John tells us: "There is much else besides that Jesus did; if all of it were put in writing, I do not think the world itself would contain the books which would have to be written" (John 21. 25).

The facts underlying this characteristic oriental paradox must be admitted. When they composed their Gospels, as *aides-mémoire* and summaries of their teaching, the inspired writers had to leave aside more than one of the Master's sayings. To reproduce *in extenso* three crowded years of teaching, both public and private, was an impossibility.[2]

There is a further interesting point: St Paul himself quotes words of Jesus which can nowhere be found in the four Gospels. For instance, in one of the sermons recorded in the Acts of the Apostles, we read: "Remembering the words spoken by the Lord Jesus himself, it is more blessed to give than to receive" (Acts 20. 35).

These words of our Lord are not of less authority than those actually found in the Gospel, since they are part of the inspired Scriptures. And there can be no question that they have the authentic ring of the words of Jesus. We have only to remember the sublime and truly divine paradox of such a saying as: "If a man is rich, gifts will be made to him: if he is poor, even the little he has will be taken away from him" (Mark 4. 25).[3] And again: "He who tries to save his life will lose it; it is the man who

---

[2] Especially as the apostles, however zealously they listened to Christ, unlike modern journalists, had not noted down his words.

[3] That is, God will greatly reward him who makes the most of his talents.

loses his life for my sake, that will save it" (Luke 9. 24).

These sentences, unquestionably, have the authentic touch. They are beyond mere literary artifice and cannot be just the product of a fertile imagination. Beyond the Tradition which has preserved them we hear the voice of Christ.

Can we say the same of all the sayings which have come down to us outside the inspired writings, through the medium of the oral teaching?

STUDY OF THE UNRECORDED SAYINGS

There are a great number of these unrecorded sayings of Jesus, by which we mean those which have not found a place in the inspired writings. They are more properly called the *Agrapha,* a Greek word, meaning the words of Jesus "not written" in the inspired writings.

These agrapha are to be found scattered among the extensive literature which grew up alongside the Gospel in the first days of Christianity. Scholars have drawn up a list of them; their origins are very varied. Some are included in ancient copies of the Gospels which the Church did not accept as her received text. They are also found in the writings of the Fathers (i.e. bishops and teachers of the first centuries), or in the apocryphal gospels. Lastly a number have been found in ancient papyri recently brought to light in Egypt where the message of Jesus was taken at a very early date.

All these witnesses of primitive oral Tradition have been made the subject of learned investigation. We shall give a few specimens of the sayings of Jesus that have been preserved, trying to assess their degree of authenticity.

COPIES OF THE GOSPELS

When the four canonical Gospels were written, the various communities procured the text of them in order to make a number of copies. It would be surprising if there were no variations in these. We know that manuscripts are by their nature liable to all sorts of vagaries. Copyists, either being distracted, forget words and phrases; or from preconceived ideas correct the text, and insert additions. Hence the number of "variants" between the manuscripts. The Church had to compare these variants very carefully to establish what is called the *Textus receptus*.

This was a laborious task, and by the third century Origen was saying: "It is quite obvious that there are today many variants in the manuscripts, either through the negligence of copyists or the perverse tendency of some to correct the text." [4]

There is an allusion to the grave tampering with the text by heretics, who selected from the Gospel passages which favoured their tenets. But it must be admitted that corrections and adaptations were made quite legitimately. At the beginning the Christian communities received Christ's message with more attention to its spirit than to the letter. For them the matter of supreme importance was fidelity to the Testament of Jesus. In a civilization in which oral teaching was usual it will be understood that a particular saying of Jesus when committed to writing may have been given in some places a particular stamp, and that certain manuscripts may have preserved fragments of traditions unknown to others.

This is the case with the celebrated incident of the woman taken in adultery, of which we read in St John's Gospel (8. 11). This episode is not found in any manu-

[4] Commentary on St Matthew, 25. 14.

script earlier than the fifth century. At that date it appeared in a well authenticated manuscript, the Codex Bezae.[5] This manuscript, a late arrival in the West, in Greek and Latin, was possibly of Egyptian origin, and anterior to the time when the content of the Gospels was entirely fixed. On historical evidence the Church has judged that the pericope of the woman taken in adultery was a fragment of oral tradition of sufficient authority to be traced back to St John through the Churches of Asia where he had preached.[6]

On the other hand the Church has not retained another addition of this same *Codex Bezae,* because it does not offer sufficient guarantee of authenticity. It is a judgement pronounced by Jesus on the matter of the Sabbath: "At that time Jesus seeing a man working on the Sabbath said to him: man, if you know what you are doing, blessed are you. But if you do not know, you are accursed and a transgressor of the Law."

In these words Jesus declares that the Jewish law of rest is abolished: to violate it was not a sin for a convinced Christian, though it remained such for the unconverted Jew. While it is perfectly sound in doctrine, can we say that it was actually uttered by Jesus? Although it is true that in the Gospel Christ shows himself as "Lord of the Sabbath" (Luke 6. 5) we have no reason to believe that this abrogation took effect in his own life time. It was St Paul and the later reflection of the Christian conscience which concluded that while Jesus held

[5] A manuscript found by Theodore Beza (1562) at the Monastery of St Irenaeus of Lyons: it is called a "codex" because it is not rolled, but composed of leaves bound at the edge, like our modern books.

[6] Eusebius of Caesarea, at the beginning of the fourth century, definitely states that the narrative in question is already found in the "Interpretations of the Words of the Lord" of Papias, a disciple of the Apostle John, about 130.

the Sabbath in esteem he had yet abrogated it in favour of the rest of the Sunday, the day of his Resurrection. This sentence then would appear to be an addition of the first generation of the Christian era.

Examples could be multiplied, but all prove that when the Gospels were copied there were certain traditions current embodying authentic sayings of Jesus, not found either in the Synoptics or St John. The majority of these variants called for a choice; they did all offer equal guarantees and, especially, added nothing substantial to the message of Jesus. They remain of interest as illustrating in many places the Received Text, and revealing the freedom of expression of the initial Gospel tradition.

THE WRITINGS OF THE FATHERS

Besides these manuscripts of the Gospels, it is in the writings of the Fathers of the Church that we find the greatest number of these agrapha.

The Fathers of the Church are so called because they were the guardians of its infancy. The greater number, bishops and heads of the Christian communities, were successors of the apostles, consecrated by them. Towards the end of his life, St Paul confided his apostolic charge to his disciple Timothy in these words:

> Fan the flame of that special grace which God kindled in thee, when my hands were laid upon thee. . . . By the power of the Holy Spirit who dwells in us, be true to thy high trust. . . . Thou hast learned, from many who can witness to it, the doctrine which I hand down; give it into the keeping of men thou canst trust, men who will know how to teach it to others besides themselves (2 Tim. 1. 6, 14; 2. 2).

This apostolic continuity was to be perpetuated in the hierarchy of the Church. And we must not forget that the first Fathers of the Church could pass on, one to the other, part of the hitherto unpublished teaching of Jesus. Papias, bishop of Hierapolis, at the beginning of the second century, had oral testimony of the teaching of St John through the aged bishop of Smyrna, Polycarp, who had been his disciple in Asia Minor. Towards the end of the century in Gaul, St Irenaeus, bishop of Lyons, was still in touch with the age of the oral tradition of the Gospel: in early life he lived with Polycarp, from whom he learnt much about John, and consequently about Jesus.

We can be assured that until about the third century, the Fathers felt themselves linked in continuity with the oral teaching of the Apostles. So it is not without interest to find coming from their pens fragments of tradition which may well go back to Christ. Certain sayings which they attribute to Christ have an unmistakable ring of the Gospel. For instance, according to St Clement of Rome, pope and martyr of the first century, Jesus said: "in the measure that you are kind, others will be to you." [7]

And in another letter falsely attributed to him, but which may be even earlier, Jesus is said to have declared: "If you are one with me and recline in my bosom, yet do not my words, I will cast you forth." [8]

This sentence is certainly semitic in style and reminiscent of St John. The expression "to recline in someone's bosom," indicates the intimacy of guests, who in ancient times took their meal lying side by side on the same couch. The Gospel notices the love of St John for Jesus in similar terms: "Jesus had one disciple, whom he loved, who was now sitting with his head against Jesus' breast" (John 13. 23).

As to the precise meaning of this sentence, we must notice the warning against an altogether too external love,

[7] Clement of Rome, Epistle 13. 2.
[8] Pseudo-Clement, II Cor. 4. 5.

which will not aim at carrying out the wishes of the beloved. Jesus one day reproached his disciples for this:
"You call me, Master, Master, and will not do what I bid
you" (Luke 6. 46).

In the middle of the second century we find in St Justin
this prophecy of Jesus on the future of his Church: "There
will be schisms and heresies." [9] This logion is similar to
the rebuke uttered by St Paul to the Corinthians: "There
are divisions among you . . . parties there must needs
be among you, so that those who are of true metal may
be distinguished from the rest" (1 Cor. 11. 18-19).

With the third and fourth centuries the distance from
Christ increases. The oral teaching of the apostles and
their immediate disciples is silenced. The sayings of Jesus
which are encountered in a letter or doctrinal treatise must
be put to more careful proof. Obviously, a choice must be
made and it is no easy matter. Some of the logia are quite
impossible: others, whose origins are not easily identified,
are not out of harmony with the Gospels.

The celebrated apologist Tertullian, who died about
230, put these profound words on the lips of Jesus: "No
one can come to the Kingdom of heaven, unless he has
passed through temptation." [10] This may be merely a variant of the Gospel parable: "The kingdom of heaven has
opened to force; and the forceful are even now making it
their prize" (Matt. 11. 12).

Tertullian gives us another gem from the mouth of
Jesus: "When you have seen your brother, you have seen
your Lord." [11] There could be no better summary of the
new Law of Christ. This logion at once reminds us of what
St John never ceases to repeat in his Epistles: "If a man
boasts of loving God, while he hates his own brother, he

[9] Dial: Trypho XXXV.
[10] *De Baptismo* 20.
[11] *De Oratione,* 26.

is a liar. He has seen his brother, and has no love for him; what love can he have for the God he has never seen?" (1 John 4. 20). Origen, the Alexandrian thinker, who died in 255, mentions a saying of Jesus which has a Semitic flavour: "The Saviour himself said: he who is near me is near fire; he who is far from me, is far from the kingdom." [12]

This sentence, which colours the image of the Kingdom with that of fire, reminds us of the Gospel, where Jesus came to inaugurate the Kingdom of God on earth by baptism, "with the Holy Ghost and with fire" (Matt. 3. 11), the fire of the judgement which even now condemns the unbelieving and saves the believers (John 3. 17-8).

Clement of Alexandria, a Greek Father, reputed for his writings, also quoted words of Jesus, of which the drift is easy to penetrate. Here is the first: "My mystery is for me and those of my house." [13] Christ used similar words in the Gospels, for did he not reserve the secret of his message for the apostles alone? "It is granted to you to know the secrets of God's kingdom, but not to these others" (Matt. 13. 11).

But the mission of the divine Revealer was in no sense clouded by any element of esoterism. The mass of his hearers could not understand him because their hearts were hardened. More than once the Master was obliged to explain the profound sense of his parables to the apostles themselves.

Less enigmatic in depth and form and very widely distributed (in all it is found thirty-seven times among several of the Fathers) is the counsel of the Lord to spiritual prudence: "Be wise in your dealings: hold fast to what is good, but reject all that appears evil."

It is remarkable that such different pens as those of

[12] *Homilia in Jer.,* 20. 3.
[13] *Stromata* 5. 10.

Origen, Clement of Alexandria and Basil of Caesarea, from the second to the fourth centuries, should have quoted these words as the authentic sayings of Jesus. Is it possible for this tradition to go back to the apostles, and ultimately to Christ? Here, as elsewhere, it is difficult to decide definitely. Perhaps it is only an echo of the Gospel phrase: "Be on your guard against false prophets who come to you in sheep's clothing . . . you will know them by the fruits they yield" (Matt. 7. 15-6); or a similar warning given by St John: "Not all prophetic spirits, brethren, deserve your credence; you must put them to the test to see whether they come from God. Many false prophets have made their appearance in the world" (1 John 4. 1).

What are we to conclude from these free quotations of the sayings of Jesus, gleaned from the Fathers? That it is possible to find true "historical sayings," transmitted on the fringe of the Gospels, by the living and continuous voice of oral Tradition, which were not published in the New Testament. But as we shall shortly show, these fragments of tradition have not the guarantee of truth of the words of the Gospel, which rest on the personal witness of the apostles.

THE APOCRYPHAL GOSPELS

What we have just said is confirmed by a fact that is now well established. The Fathers, though they did not always indicate the source of the words of Jesus which they quoted, did not hesitate to draw frequently from the apocryphal gospels which came into their hands. Some of these gospels, which were very widely distributed, had acquired a certain authority from the fact they originated in quarters close to Christ and his apostles. Their value is mentioned in the next chapter; here are given only quotations of the sayings of Jesus that have been drawn from some of the Fathers. Origen declares, for instance: "If any one receives the gospel according to the Hebrews, the Saviour says in this gospel: a moment ago, my mother the Holy Spirit seized me by one of my hairs and carried me to the lofty mountain of Tabor." [14]

Fr Lagrange, who has studied this strange logion,[15] thinks that it is related to the temptation of Christ (Matt. 4. 8). It seems to contradict the Gospel on one point in saying that not the Devil but the power of the Holy Spirit carried Jesus to the top of the mountain. Why does Jesus call the Holy Spirit "my mother"? This is a strange idea which has no doctrinal support in Scripture. But it can be explained linguistically, for in the Aramean dialect which Jesus spoke the word spirit was in the feminine gender. We need not seek further for the origin of this title which strikes us as grotesque. Eusebius, bishop of Caesarea in Palestine in the fourth century, also found an excellent logion in the *Gospel according to the Hebrews.* Jesus speaks of the choosing of his apostles: "I choose for myself the most worthy: the most worthy are those whom the heavenly Father gives me." This saying is exactly parallel to the divine choice of which Christ speaks in the Gospel of St John: "It was not you that chose me, it was I that chose you" (John 15. 16); "I have made thy name known to the men whom thou hast entrusted to me" (John 17. 6).

The gospel of the Ebionites—we shall speak of it again —was another source of the logia of Jesus. It contained the Lord's Prayer with an interesting variant, noticed by St Jerome, the great exegete of the fourth century. Instead of the petition: "Give us this day our daily bread" (Matt.

[14] *Comm. in Joan.* 2. 12.
[15] *Revue Biblique,* 1922, pp. 171-81, 321-49.

6. 11), we have "Give us this day our bread for tomorrow."

This reading is not to be despised. It comes from the Aramean, the language spoken by Jesus[16] and even in the Greek text of St Matthew it is a plausible reading. But it seems rather to express the ideal of these "poor of God" who drew up a Gospel to suit their own taste.[17] Would Christ have wished that his followers should pray for tomorrow's bread? Hardly so, for in the commentary which he himself gives on the Lord's Prayer, Jesus says to his apostles: "I say to you, do not fret over your life, how to support it with food and drink . . . you have a Father in heaven who knows that you need them all . . . do not fret, then, over tomorrow; leave tomorrow to fret over its own needs; for today, today's troubles are enough" (Matt. 6. 25, 32, 34).

Lastly, St Epiphanius, bishop of Salamis, in Cyprus, has noticed another saying in the gospel of the Ebionites: "I have come to abolish sacrifices; if you do not refrain from sacrifice, the anger of God will continue against you." [18] This is an exaggerated form of the exhortation found in many of the prophets: "I will have mercy and not sacrifice."

Of course, Jesus came to abolish the multitude of the Jewish sacrifices which in themselves had no true worth. But he has substituted for them the sacrifice of his own divine Person. He willed that his disciples should renew for themselves this one and only efficacious sacrifice when he gave to them at the Last Supper his Body and Blood, saying to them, "Do this for a commemoration of me."

[16] The word MAHAR means "for tomorrow" in Aramaic, as St Jerome realized.

[17] See below The Gospel of the Ebionites, p. 144. (Ebionite means "poor.")

[18] Epiphanius, *Homil*. 3. 51.

The abolition of all sacrifice, which is not to be found in the express will of Christ, is attributed to him in a sectarian gospel tinged with the theories of the Essenes.[19]

What value have these borrowing of the Fathers from the apocryphal gospels current in the first centuries? Were these great thinkers mistaken about the value of their sources. If one or other of them could believe for a moment that the gospel according to the Hebrews was the Aramaic original of the Greek Gospel of St Matthew, the majority of the ecclesiastical writers knew well enough that this document, and others like it, were used only in limited circles and these of more or less sectarian views. Besides, after the second century, all accepted the four Gospels alone, recognized as the true "recollections of the Apostles," the phrase used by St Justin in his *Dialogue with Trypho the Jew* (*c.* 155), meaning by this the works of Mark, Matthew, Luke and John exclusively.

Despite the passage of time the Fathers were always ready to accept fragments of the words or actions of Jesus which might have escaped the evangelists. Their interest was motivated, at least in the two first centuries, by the actual survival of the oral teaching of the apostles. In the following centuries, the risks of error were greater. But certain writings, possessed by a particular community, could possibly go back to the apostolic age and, without possessing the authority of the canonical Gospels, could yet have preserved authentic fragments of the primitive apostolic teaching.

The Fathers ran this risk. Whatever the ultimate value of their gleanings, they are evidence of the reverence which these defenders of the faith had for all which, closely or remotely, concerned the person of Christ.

---

[19] The Jewish sect of the Essenes, living side by side with official Judaism, seems to have rejected sacrifices as too material for a religion of the heart.

THE EGYPTIAN PAPYRI

In addition to the writings of the Fathers, a final source of the unpublished sayings of Jesus endows our investigation with a certain topicality. Since the end of the nineteenth century excavations in Egypt have brought to light remains of the papyrus with which the ancient inhabitants used to wrap their mummies. This papyrus, before being employed for this purpose, was commonly used for letter writing. Their discovery is of extreme importance. It has enabled us to unearth copies of the canonical Gospels, particularly a fragment of the fourth Gospel, absolutely identical with the text received by the Church, and dated by scholars from the beginning of the second century.[20] This fragment alone proves that St John's Gospel was written early enough to have reached Egypt by 140.

But together with these most precious copies of the New Testament, the excavators have found remains of a number of other "gospels," having something in common with the inspired text, yet deviating in other ways.

Fragments of an unknown text have been discovered, especially in the regions of the Lybian desert, and on the site of the ancient Greek city of Oxyrhynchus. The manuscript fragments covered a mummy in a Christian tomb of the third century. Two scholars, Grenfell and Hunt, published in 1897 a series of seven "sayings of Jesus" which were found included in this. Each began with the formula "Jesus said" and the tone of at least two of them is worthy of Christ's utterance. Here is the first: "Lift up the stone and you shall find me: cleave in two the wood and I am there." [21]

Under a typically oriental image, this seems to be a

[20] This is the Rylands Papyrus 457.
[21] Oxyrhynchus Papyrus 1, recto 1, 6-7.

reflection on the dignity of manual labour, which far from taking us away from God, brings us to him. It is true that in the Gospels Christ made no pronouncement on the dignity of work. Perhaps it is a correction of the pessimistic proverb to be found in Ecclesiastes: "Stone crushes his foot that stone carries, and wood crushes him that wood cuts" (10. 9).

And the second fine saying put into the Saviour's mouth is this: "Where two are united, God is not separated from them: and even when there is one alone, I am with him." [22]

We find something similar in the Gospel: "Where two or three are gathered together in my name, I am there in the midst of them" (Matt. 18. 20), and again: "But when thou art praying, go into thy inner room and shut the door upon thyself, and so pray to thy Father in secret; and then thy Father, who sees what is done in secret, will reward thee" (Matt. 6. 6). But will it ever be possible to say definitely that Christ actually pronounced the words which have been buried in the sands of Egypt until this present day?

We may conclude this glance at the sayings of Jesus not included in the inspired Gospels by quoting an Arabic inscription found about 1900, where the following thought is attributed to our Lord: "This world is a bridge: pass over, but do not build your home on it." Rabbinical literature has parallels with this logion. But being quite unconnected with the Gospel, we may think that it belongs to ancient Mohammedan traditions, brought to the East by the Prophet's disciples towards the seventh century of our era.

[22] Oxyrhynchus Papyrus 1, recto 1, 8-9.

THE TARES AND THE WHEAT

The critics of the end of the nineteenth century, in the excitement of the first great biblical excavations of our time, thought for the moment that their discoveries were going to transform the traditional picture of Christ, especially the substance of his doctrine as it is revealed to us in the Gospel. In 1889, a German critic, A. Resch, produced a rich collection of the sayings of Jesus unrecorded in Scripture. But after a severe but necessary elimination had been made by J. H. Ropes in 1896 and Bauer in 1909, removing all incongruous and meaningless expressions, a remnant of about a hundred of these logia remained to be considered.

In our own days, Professor Jeremias, who has made an attentive study of this subject, has retained as authentic only about twenty of these sayings. The criterion of his judgement is very sound. There are, according to this scholar,[23] a number of sayings which were put together to serve the purpose of some heresy; false doctrines, in fact, sought formulation in the mould of the Gospel formulas to obtain a certain authority. The Gnostic heresy—of which we shall speak later—made its own gospels, and had no scruple in circulating false logia of Jesus to bolster up its theories of salvation.

And the Christian community itself, which had by then extended over the known world, and was separated by a certain distance of time from the events of the Gospel, attributed to Jesus, either by lapse of memory or want of exact knowledge, sayings which he had never uttered. Also, exaggeration, inaccurate quotations have spread

[23] Dr Joachim Jeremias: *Des mots inconnus de Jésus*, Zurich 1948.

abroad authentic sayings of Jesus, the original form of which cannot now be proved.

In any case, apart from the sayings suspect of dogmatic error, or definitely unacceptable because out of place or meaningless, there remains a substratum of sayings, of convincing content and of reasonable authenticity.

These fragments, collected with great labour from numerous writings and several centuries of Tradition, do not really enrich our knowledge of Christ and of the truth taught by him. The authenticity of the sayings mentioned above is by no means certain. Critics remain divided on the possibility of their going back to Jesus himself. They lack the authentification which the words of the Gospel enjoy or the evidence of an eyewitness of Christ within the primitive Church.

It has been pointed out that a great many of the sayings attributed to Jesus were for the most part of doubtful origin. Obviously, it must be repeated, the living, enduring voice of oral Tradition could hand down some of the deeds and sayings of Jesus which had not found a place in those necessary summaries we call the Gospels. But the Fathers of the third and fourth centuries gave their sources: most of the logia they quoted were derived from a literature of tendentious nature, which has not survived the test of time, for want of due authenticity. Even the Egyptian papyri seem to be only more or less free extracts from both the apocryphal and canonical gospels. St Irenaeus, about 180, said: "Such is the authority of the Gospels that even the heretics reverence them, and each tries to state his doctrine on the basis of this authority."

It is quite certain that from the end of the second century oral Tradition was the bearer of a good many more tares than wheat. At least, we can say that our study of the unwritten "sayings" of Jesus allows us to appreciate by contrast the great value of the Gospel text.

CHAPTER XIII

THE MESSAGE OF JESUS

AND THE SECTS

It is scarcely possible to believe the tremendous literary activity which was stirred up in the world by the appearance of the Gospels. When Christian communities spread not only to Asia, but to Africa and then to Europe, an immense literature about Jesus and his doctrine came into being. While the Church copied and recopied the narrative of the apostles, following the fashion certain communities began to do likewise, but at the same time suiting their own ideas and customs.

Thus there was a proliferation of apocryphal gospels on more or less sectarian lines. For the ancient world in which the Gospel was preached was fundamentally religious. Against this upstart Christianity, the old religions defended their heritage, or if it suited them exploited the new religion. It was an age of syncretism, the fusion of more or less reconcilable beliefs.

Two main religious currents, one Jewish, the other Greek, attempted to annex the Gospel. The first resulted in the Judaizers, threatening the Church from within; the other, a mixture of philosophy and pagan beliefs, gave rise to Gnosticism, threatening the Church from without.

THE JUDAIZERS

It is sometimes too easily forgotten that Christianity was born of Judaism, as the young shoot from an old trunk. This is indisputable. Jesus was a Jew: he was born, bred and lived in Palestine. His teaching is grafted on the Old Testament, the pure fruit of the Israelite faith. He said himself: "I have not come to set aside the law and the prophets; but to bring them to perfection." The Son of God revealed himself as the Messiah, the final prophet of Israel and the fulfiller of the divine promises made to the Chosen People. It is not surprising, therefore, that the first Christians were converted Jews.

But owing to their origin and the strong affection which they retained for their ancestral faith, the Jewish converts —the Judaizers—had great difficulty in assimilating the new message of Jesus. They wanted to retain many of the Jewish rites and customs and to impose them on Gentile converts. In doing so, they incurred the risk of turning Christianity into an additional Jewish sect. The very existence of the infant Catholic Church was at stake. Jesus died for all men. Paul proclaimed that there is neither Jew nor Gentile, but that all were called to faith in the same Lord, and he had to fight for the achievement of this principle. The mother Church of Jerusalem was entirely formed of those who had been Jews, and Peter and James were to a certain extent under the influence of this prevalent Jewish mentality. This misunderstanding was only eliminated by the work of Paul, the Apostle of the Gentiles, at the Council of Jerusalem, the first ecumenical council, in 49. Afterwards there was agreement on the point: the rites which had been made superfluous by the sacraments of the new dispensation were never again to be imposed on non-Jewish converts (Acts 15).

Some little time had to elapse, however, before the decisions of this council could be applied to all the Jewish Christian communities settled both in Palestine and the Dispersion. Some of these did not entirely fall into line with the universal outlook animating the apostles and their successors. Jealously attached to their own traditions, these communities adapted the Gospel to suit their own ideas. Here and there appeared Gospels which, if not heretical, were at least very tendentious.

THE GOSPEL OF THE NAZARENES

In the fourth century, Epiphanius, the Bishop of Salamis, mentions the Nazarenes, a Judaizing sect which was flourishing in his time. These folk assumed the title borne by Jesus (Matt. 2. 23) and practised the chief Jewish rites: circumcision, the Sabbath, etc. More Jewish than Christian, they connected their traditions with the most Jewish of the Evangelists, St Matthew. Epiphanius remarks: "They possess a Gospel according to St Matthew, written in Hebrew and very complete." [1] Was this really the Gospel of that apostle? As this has come down to us in Greek, not in Hebrew, we cannot be in the least certain. Could it be the original version? The Fathers thought so. St Jerome stated: "The Hebrew Gospel (of St Matthew) is still extant in the library of Caesarea . . . I had the chance of transcribing it. It was given to me by the Nazarenes, who use this work at Beroea in Syria." [2]

This master of exegesis tells us that he made, for his own use, a Greek and Latin translation of the manuscript which is called "the gospel according to the Hebrews,"

---

[1] Epiphanius: *Panarion*, 29. 8.
[2] Jerome: *De viribus illustribus* 3; we may add that the scholars have given up hope of ever finding again the Hebrew original of the first Gospel.

that is, according to these Christians of the Hebrew tongue, the Jewish Christians of Syria. The gospel according to the Hebrews has not come down to us in the full text. We only know it from short extracts, made by the Fathers of the third and fourth centuries. Fr Lagrange, the founder of the École Biblique at Jerusalem has studied them.[3]

Taken together the extracts do not reveal a strictly heretical view, but the text has been changed to suit the taste of these Christians who had not entirely broken with Judaism. Thus, on the baptism of Jesus, "In the gospel which the Nazarenes still use," writes St Jerome, "there is this story: the mother of Jesus and his brethren said to him: John the Baptist instituted baptism for the remission of sins. Let us go and be baptized by him. But he answered: where have I sinned that I need his baptism? Believe me when I speak thus, for indeed it is so." [4]

It appears that this little episode is intended to dispel the scandal caused to the Jews and the Judaizers by the fact that Jesus by accepting baptism from John—as the Gospel tells us—ranges himself alongside sinners. But actually Christ's action must be explained quite differently. It was revealed to John the Baptist at the baptism that Jesus was the Messiah, the divine Envoy sent by the Spirit to proclaim the news of salvation (cf. John 1. 29-34). The Nazarenes were alone in not understanding this perfectly clear text of the Gospel.

An event in the appearances of the risen Christ shows an even more marked Jewish tendency. Here is the fragment, from Jerome:

When the Lord had given his winding sheet to the High Priest's servant,[5] he went to James and appeared to him

[3] *Revue Biblique*, 1922, pp. 171-81, 321-49.
[4] *Contra Pelag.* 3. 2.
[5] No other authority mentions this incident of Jesus handing his winding sheet to the High Priest's servant.

first. For James had sworn that he would eat bread no
more after he had drunk of the Lord's chalice till he saw
him risen from the dead. . . . Then the Lord took bread,
blessed it and broke it and gave it to James the Just,
saying, my child, eat this bread, for the Son of Man is
risen from the dead.

According to this passage, the risen Lord first appeared
to James, the apostle who became the head of the mother
community of Jerusalem, after the departure of Peter
(Acts 21. 17-18), and was known for his sympathies for
the Judaizers (Gal. 2. 12). To single out this apostle,
rather than Peter, the Prince of the Apostles, and head
of the Universal Church, was an indication that in this
Church there was a predominance of Jewish converts. The
Nazarenes were still in the majority in the fourth century.
But against them was the apostolic witness of St Paul who
had written to the Corinthians in 55 7: "The chief message I handed on to you, as it was handed to me . . .
that he was seen by Cephas (Peter), then by the eleven
apostles . . . then he was seen by James, then by all the
apostles" (in the general sense of disciples: 1 Cor. 15.
3-7).

The gospel of the Nazarenes gives the impression of a
readjustment of the text, corrected and commented upon
like the Jewish targums. Although no formal heresy is to
be found in it, this gospel was nevertheless that of a particular sect. It is quite possible that its appearance ante-
dates the Gospel of St Matthew *in Greek,* and that a group
of Jewish Christians in the Church were anxious to possess their Gospel in Hebrew. Everything, however, leads
us to conclude that they did not succeed in this. In the
fourth century this Hebrew gospel was only used by a
local and extremely restricted sect; it never achieved the
status of an inspired Gospel.

THE GOSPEL OF THE EBIONITES

In addition to the Nazarenes, the early Church knew another Jewish Christian sect, the Ebionites.

These people, whose name in Hebrew means "the poor," were also sprung from Judaism, set out to realize the ideal of spiritual poverty which the prophets had cultivated among an élite of the Chosen People. The Ebionites certainly saw in Jesus one who realized their ideal—the ideal Poor Man, but they had not accepted all the implications of his message. Rather they continued under the influence of the Law in certain beliefs and practices.

Again it is St Epiphanius who describes these sectaries. From him we learn that the Ebionites, together with special rites, more or less based on the Christian mysteries, professed a creed that was quite unorthodox. They held that Jesus was an ordinary man, born like everyone else. He owed his title of "Son of God" only by virtue of a special adoption. On him had fallen from on high a "Power" called "Christ," which by its very name gave him a divine consecration. In short, the Ebionites professed the adoptionist heresy, which taught that Jesus was the Son of God only by "adoption" and not by nature.[6]

The gospel of the Ebionites was known to the Fathers. Once again it is Epiphanius who informs us: "The Ebionites accept the gospel of Matthew which they use, and call 'according to the Hebrews.' But this gospel of theirs is incomplete, falsified and mutilated." [7] Presumably this sect had fundamentally the same text as the Nazarenes,

[6] The strict monotheism of the Jews forbade them to accept the fact of Persons in God.
[7] Epiphanius, *Panarion.* 30. 3, 13.

but unlike these latter, the Ebionite gospel is described as mutilated, and especially corrupted.

A few quotations prove this. Here is the narrative of the call of the apostles: "When Jesus had come to Capharnaum he entered the house of Simon (?) and opening his mouth said to him: as I came to the Lake of Tiberias I chose John and James, the sons of Zebedee, and Simon (Peter) and Andrew." [8]

We can see here an instance of the preference accorded to James over Peter, the prince of the apostles. The same prejudices obtain here as among the Nazarenes. But the canonical Greek Gospel of Matthew tells us quite definitely, of the same episode: "As he walked by the sea of Galilee, Jesus saw two brethren, Simon who is called Peter, and his brother Andrew . . . then he went further on and saw two others that were brethren, James the son of Zebedee and his brother John. . . . He called to them . . . whereupon they dropped their nets . . . and followed him" (Matt. 4. 18-22).

The Ebionite gospel is not only a deliberate corruption of the Gospel narrative, but also furnishes evidence of practices half Jewish and half Christian: "In addition to the daily ritual bath they have an initiation rite of baptism, and each year celebrate various mysteries in imitation of the Church and the faithful." [9]

We know also from a study of the logion on the condemnation of sacrifices,[10] that the Ebionites appeared to reject this means of communion with God. This is confirmed in the passage dealing with the Sacrifice of the Pasch: "The apostles said to Jesus: when do you wish us to prepare the Pasch? He answered them, do you think that I wish to eat meat with you as the Pasch?" [11]

[8] Epiphanius, *Panarion*. 30. 13.
[9] Epiphanius, *Panarion*, 30. 16.
[10] See p. 133.
[11] Epiphanius, op. cit. 30. 28. 4.

This disconcerting reply is far removed from the "longing" shown by Jesus (Luke 22. 15) to eat the Jewish Pasch, which he was to replace in the course of the meal by the sacrifice of his Body and Blood. In this matter the Ebionites professed what is termed the Encratite heresy: the contempt for the use of marriage and rejection of that of meat.[12]

It is obvious that the Ebionite gospel radically changed the most definite sources of the Gospel Tradition. While the Nazarenes were simply attached to Jewish customs, the Ebionites formed a heretical sect among the Jewish Christians.

GNOSTICISM

Threatened from within and without, the early Church had not only from within to break off from the Jewish world, but from without to contend with the pagan world, a world then in full religious vigour. Even Greek philosophy, the mistress of reason and logic, accepted the wildest lucubrations of oriental mysticism. The Near East and the Western shore of the Mediterranean knew a strange mixture of different religions, warring philosophies and magic cults.

Shortly after Christianity, there arose in Asia Minor one of those mystery religions called Gnosis or the Knowledge of Salvation. In the second century it enjoyed an extraordinary success in Egypt, before spreading throughout the Roman Empire. It was in the country of the Nile, the traditional home of religious ferment, that this new religion grievously contaminated the purity of the Christian faith. In Alexandria famous teachers—Basilidees, Carpocrates, Valentinian—founded their schools. The Gnostics, "those who know," proliferated in sects and systems, with many variations of doctrine.

[12] Encratism was the practice of a morbid asceticism.

Contrary to the Gospel this heresy maintained an op-
position between God and the created world. The supreme
Deity, all good and perfect, is quite unconnected with an
evil creation, which is the unsuccessful labour of an ignorant and malign divinity, a monstrous power, which
with the cosmic forces, tyrannically rules over the world.
In this lower world Fate and Destiny (personified by the
Archontes, that is the planets) hold man down and en-
chain him. He suffers in the prison of the body. But his
soul, in secret and all unknown to him happily conceals
a luminous fragment of the higher world. Salvation lies
in the liberation of the heavenly particle from its impris-
onment in fallen matter. The saviour can be nothing else
than a spirit from the supreme deity, which will secretly
enlighten him that he belongs to a higher world. This
revelation is *Gnosis:* Knowledge, which a man receives
in a hidden way, that he belongs to a higher sphere. It
unfolds to him the despotic wickedness of creation and of
the body which holds him captive, and also gives him the
strength to rise above the cosmic Powers which surround
the world.

When, in this perspective, the Gnostics make of Jesus,
from among innumerable rivals, the Saviour, they do not
consider him as a god incarnate, but as a subtle spirit, who
is free of all the restraints of matter. Salvation does not
come through his death and resurrection (which are unthinkable), but simply from the secret revelation of the
world beyond which he brings.

AN UNKNOWN LIBRARY

Until the present time the Fathers were our chief source
of information about this pernicious heresy. A contemporary, St Irenaeus, in his work "Against Heresies," became
the outstanding defender of the Church against Gnosti-

cism. We may legitimately wonder whether the heresy was either so widespread or so important as to demand such a magisterial doctrinal refutation. Yet an amazing discovery has recently confirmed both the extent of Gnosticism, and the value of the information adduced by ecclesiastical writers.

In 1947—at the same time that the Dead Sea scrolls were brought to light—a library of Gnostic writings was discovered in Egypt. The discovery caused no stir, and yet it inaugurated a new stage in our knowledge of this mysterious Gnosticism. Thirteen volumes, comprising forty-nine different treatises, were dug up from the sands of Nag-Hammadi, somewhat to the south of Luxor in Upper Egypt. The Egyptian museum at Cairo has acquired the collection which is now being examined. This gigantic task puts us in possession of works of which hitherto we knew the existence only by hearsay. Furthermore, it gives us forty-four secret books, wholly unknown hitherto, belonging to various categories: revelations of a purely Gnostic type, Christian speculation tainted with Gnosticism, etc.

Further mention will be made of certain of these writings which took the form of Christian literature at the time, such as the "acts" of John, of Peter and of Paul; the apocalypses, of Peter, of Paul or of James.[13] To confine ourselves to the "gospels" or related writings, we mention: the gospel of the Egyptians, a gospel according to Thomas, according to Matthias, the gospel of Truth, the Sophia (Wisdom) of Jesus. We cannot discuss all these texts, especially as their publication is not yet finished. A resumé can, however, be given of some of them; here are mentioned particularly the various gospels in which authentic Christian belief is contaminated by Gnostic ideas.

According to one tradition, which totally ignores the existence of the four canonical Gospels, Jesus had en-

[13] See Chapter XV.

trusted the task of putting his teaching into writing to the apostles Philip, Thomas and Matthias only, which is the reason for the circulation of a gospel of each of these pseudo-sacred writers.

THE GOSPEL OF PHILIP

This is nothing more than a vague treatise in which Christian ideas are mixed up with some very questionable theories. The words and deeds of Jesus are given a Gnostic interpretation. It is through the sacraments that man, mysteriously united to the Spirit as by a carnal union, will escape from this mortal condition and be freed from this evil world. Baptism by fire and water is an "anointing with light" from above: the Eucharist is thus treated: "It is the chalice of prayer: there is the wine, there is the water, which is made ready like blood, over which we give thanks. It is full of the Holy Spirit: it is the food of the perfect man. When we drink of it, we receive in ourselves this perfect man, the living water, a body with which we must clothe ourselves."

THE GOSPEL OF THOMAS

Known already to the Fathers, and described about 230 as "apocryphal" by Hippolytus of Rome, it is not what we call a gospel at all. It is a collection of more than a hundred logia, a number of which were those found at Oxyrhynchus. The work begins in an esoteric fashion: "Here are the secret words which the Living Jesus spoke, which Didymus Judas Thomas has written down."

There is nothing original in these secret words, and they are more or less similar to our Gospels. About half however are entirely new. The collection is marred by some of these latter, as for instance the 103rd and last:

"Simon Peter said to the Apostles: Let Mary depart from our midst, for women are not worthy of our life. Jesus answered: Behold, I will turn her into a male, so that she may become a living spirit as you men: every woman who has become a male will enter into the Kingdom of heaven.

THE GOSPEL OF MATTHIAS

Clement of Alexandria had already quoted from this work certain "secret traditions" with a strongly Gnostic tinge. The reputed author, who replaced Judas among the twelve (Acts 1. 21-6), ascribes to Christ some very sectarian and unbecoming sentiments.

For instance, after the resurrection, Salome, one of the holy women of the Gospel, asks Jesus: "How long shall death exercise its power?" Jesus answers: "As long as women beget children."

"Then I have done rightly in having no children."

To which our Saviour makes the disconcerting answer: "Eat every herb, but not one which is bitter. . . . I have come to destroy woman's work."

According to this, then, Jesus in no uncertain terms condemned the work of the flesh.

MYSTERY GOSPELS

There may be a few good grains from the Gospel tradition scattered among the treatises we have just mentioned. But what can be said of works which, while passing for Christian, impart a purely Gnostic doctrine?

Such is the case with the "Wisdom of Jesus." This purports to be a dialogue between Jesus and the apostles after the resurrection. While the latter are fruitlessly discussing the secrets of God and creation, Jesus appeared

to them as an angel of light and explained to them in a
mysterious jargon the creation of the world:

> The Son of Man united himself to Wisdom, his com-
> panion, and begot a great androgynous light; its male name
> is Saviour, Creator of all things; its female name is Sophia,
> the begetter of all things. Everyone coming into the world
> is sent by her as a fragment of the Kingdom of the light of
> the All-Powerful, etc . . .

With the *"Sacred Book of the Great Invisible Spirit"*
we are taken completely into the realm of myth. It is also
called "the *gospel of the Egyptians*," "a book written by
God, sacred and hidden."

This has been hitherto confused with the "gospel according to the Egyptians," a work known to the Fathers,
but different. This treats, in short, of a revelation put into
the mouth of the "Great Seth," the third son of Adam
(Gen. 4. 25). Seth represents the Father of the "race of
the perfect," and he was thought to retain the first divine
spark which was imprisoned in this world by the cosmic
Powers. The "Sethites" say they are known to him to be
delivered. We may note in passing that some Gnostic sects
put themselves under the patronage of the least reputable
of the Old Testament characters. If some rely on Seth,
others rely on Cain the murderer of Abel (Gen. 4. 8):
these are the Cainites. Then there are others, the Ophites
who look to no other than the Serpent driven from Paradise (Gen. 3. 1). Apart from Christ, often appropriated
as one of them, the prophets of the new religion could
not be borrowed from either the Jewish or Christian religion; to the Gnostics, the Divine Creator of the Old
Testament was evil, his law and his prophets had only
enslaved "the Chosen ones of Gnosis" to the Powers of
this world.

We can see the aberration to which the "revelations" of
this mysterious science of salvation led. Please God their

authors may not be taken as oracles. A final specimen of their ravings is given in the third century by the *Pistis Sophia*. Jesus teaches his disciples the Gnosis:

> Until then he had not told them of all the emanations or places of the great Invisible Spirit, of the threefold powers, of the twenty-four invisible ones, and of their eons, habitations and rank: he had not spoken of those unbegotten, self-begotten, and created, their stars, their divisions, their archontes, their principalities, their archangels, their leaders, their rites.[14]

It must be acknowledged that the adherents of Gnosticism, with their secret books, their hidden revelations reserved for the initiated very quickly gave the impression of obstinately lagging behind the times. By the middle of the second century the four canonical Gospels were known and received in all parts of the ancient world. So that there was a revelation of salvation brought by Christ which was addressed to all men, without mystery or secret cult. The truth of the Gospel was clear in a very different way from the esoteric teaching of the Gnostics.

It can be said that Gnosticism, from the start, was a regression of the mind in its search for Truth. It would not have survived till the Middle Ages (among the Manicheans and the sects of Islam) if it had not borrowed the best of its teaching from orthodox Christianity. The infant Church never allowed herself to be seduced by Gnosticism. St Paul, while he may present Christ's message in analogous language, had already rejected the foolishness of Gnosticism: "Must we not say that God has turned our worldly wisdom to folly? . . . Here are the Jews asking for signs and wonders, here are the Greeks intent on their philosophy, but what we preach is Christ crucified, to the Jews a discouragement, to the Gentiles a mere folly" (1 Cor. 1. 20-3).

[14] *Pistis Sophia,* from translation by C. Schmidt (Berlin Corpus).

CHAPTER XIV

APOCRYPHA

OF THE DEATH AND

RESURRECTION OF JESUS

THE GOSPEL OF PETER

At a distance of twenty centuries it is difficult to understand how extremely perturbing were the death and resurrection of Jesus to his contemporaries. A scandal to the Jews, quite meaningless to the pagans, the cross was indeed the great sign of contradiction. In one place it stirred up doubts and objections, in another a lively curiosity. There was a desire to reconsider the facts and to reconstruct the trial of Jesus in a highly controversial spirit.

The apocryphal literature set out to refashion the Gospel narrative in its own way so as to provide a version revised and corrected according to partisan views.

One account, the gospel of Peter, is interesting here on account of its venerable antiquity; it is a work which is ascribed to the years 120 to 130, thus taking us back to within scarcely fifty years of the appearance of the Gospel narratives of the Passion. Until the nineteenth century it was only known by name and by rare quotations in the Fathers. But in 1886 the Frenchman Bouriant discovered the fragment Akhmin in Upper Egypt.

This manuscript fragment has given us the conclusion of a Passion narrative, with the entire story of the crucifixion and resurrection. We know from Eusebius of Caesarea that at the end of the second century, Scipio, bishop of Antioch, forbade the reading of this gospel on account of its more than doubtful authenticity. The work claimed special credit by using the name of the Prince of the Apostles himself. Scholars have examined this fragment of Akhmin and demonstrated its falsity. It is simply a radical recasting of the Gospel narratives: more than a hundred changes have been noted in only fifty-seven verses of the manuscript. We shall explain shortly why pseudo-Peter has taken such liberties with the Gospel text. The author has sought to bring home to the Jews the crime they have committed against Jesus and at the same time by a new narrative to establish the divinity of Christ.

The Trial of Jesus

The canonical Gospels have preserved for us the story of Jesus' trial with the most minute care. There was a double trial: the religious one before the Sanhedrin, the assembly of the Jewish priests and scribes: the political one before the civil authorities, Herod, the governor of Judaea, and Pontius Pilate, the Roman governor.

We know how Jesus was dragged from one tribunal to another, as a religious hoax and as a political agitator. Only the Roman representative, charged with preserving the peace of the Empire could pronounce sentence of death. Pilate could not legally condemn Jesus. If in the last resort the accused was killed it was due to the cowardice of this judge in handing him over to his Jewish persecutors.

In the apocryphal narrative this moving story of the Gospel has undergone a disconcerting and theatrical deformation. The story, the beginning of which is unfortunately missing, opens abruptly at the judicial tribunal when the verdict is pronounced. Here is the passage: "None of the Jews washed their hands, neither Herod or any of the judges. As they would not wash their hands, Pilate went away. Then King Herod ordered them to seize the Lord, saying: all that I have commanded you to do to him, you must do" (Gospel of Peter 1. 1, 2).

A curious scene whose improbability is obvious. First, this meeting of the civil and religious authorities in one session, a meeting which has no foundation at all in historical traditions faithfully handed down by the Gospel. And then this washing of hands, rejected by the Sanhedrin, and by Herod and his judges: there is no trace of this little episode in the authentic Gospel. And lastly the sentence of death pronounced by Herod the King, when it was the right of Pilate: it is all a travesty of history! But at least we can understand the controversial purpose of the author of this false story. He is anxious to saddle the Jews with the entire responsibility for the death of Jesus, thus completely exonerating Pilate.

It is significant that another apocryphal writer of the fourth century has tried to exonerate Pilate by incriminating the Jews alone. The "gospel of Nicodemus," known also under the name of "Acts of Pilate," shows Caesar's procurator as sympathetic to Jesus. Despite the duties of his office, he is made to take Christ's part openly. His washing of his hands at the end of the trial indicated purely and simply a sentence of acquittal.

The "gospel of Peter" does not go as far as that, but the underlying spirit is the same. Pilate, by his abrupt departure, disassociates himself completely from the ultimate verdict: he leaves to the Jews, and to Herod in particular, the responsibility of condemning Jesus.

Obviously, in the inspired Gospel the Jews, the accusers of Jesus, are those who incur the greatest guilt for his condemnation. But Pilate's record is not unsullied. Certainly at first he treated the accused in a way that does him credit. After his repeated questions he is convinced that Jesus is guilty of no crime: "It is plain that he has done nothing which deserves death."

But we must deeply regret that in spite of the fact that he alone could pronounce capital punishment, Pilate did not exert himself to the uttermost to save Jesus. On the contrary, we see this adroit official, while exonerating himself before public opinion, handing over the innocent man. Pilate's hand-washing becomes here a culpable act, which, far from excusing him, makes him an accomplice of those who demand the blood of "the Just One." The evangelists are quite explicit: after emphasizing that this high Roman official knew that Jesus was entirely innocent, they yet conclude: "Jesus he scourged, and gave him up to be crucified" (Matt. 27. 26).

The Crucifixion

In their narrative of the crucifixion of Jesus, the four Evangelists have been particularly attentive to the person sentenced to death. They have most carefully preserved the last words of Jesus, the peace of his last breath. They scarcely mention, only as the background, the mourning of nature which marks the hour of Satan, the Prince of Darkness. "From the sixth hour onwards there was darkness over all the earth until the ninth hour" (Matt. 27, 45).

The gospel of Peter has reversed the perspective. The resignation of Christ on the cross is of less interest than the anxiety and terror aroused among the Jews by the darkness in the middle of the day: "It was mid-day when darkness enveloped the whole of Judaea; the Jews were troubled and feared that the sun had gone down because Jesus still lived: it is written for them that the sun should not set on a dead criminal" (verses 15-16).

The author is here satirizing the Jews who, untroubled in conscience at the greatest of all crimes, are gravely disturbed by a trifling disobedience to the Law (leaving a dead criminal during the night). There is an element of the tragically comic at the sight of these scrupulous folk, in the belief that night has fallen, going round with lanterns, yet still stumbling; and then when Christ is dead, rejoicing because the sun begins to shine once more. As the principal argument for his thesis, the author concludes that on this occasion "the Jews fulfilled all that was foretold and filled the measure of their sin" (verse 17).

During this interlude Jesus died on the cross. His last moments have been relegated to the background. The gospel of Peter retains only one of the words from the cross: "The Lord cried out, my power, my power, thou hast left me. Then at these words he was taken up" (verse 19). How are we to explain this deformation of the cry which Matthew and Mark had put on the lips of Christ in these words: "My God, my God, why hast thou forsaken me?" (Matt. 27. 46; Mark 15. 34).

The Jews certainly saw in this cry only a sign of weakness and a certain mark that God had left him. The author evidently wished to modify this impression by substituting for the word God the vague and impersonal mention of power: this was to make Jesus merely proclaim the loss of his vitality, or at most his superhuman power. Now this is not merely to tamper with the sacred Text, but to reveal a complete misunderstanding of its true meaning. This cry of Jesus never indicated that he felt that he was deserted by God. In the first place it was simply a quotation of the opening words of Psalm 22. A Semite was accustomed to refer to a book, text or prayer by quoting its opening words. Jesus, then, was referring to the whole of Psalm 22, and in so doing applied to himself not only the complaint of the suffering Just One, but the expression of radiant hope with

which the psalm concludes. And the other utterances of
Christ on the cross are sufficient evidence that Jesus remained absolutely at one with the Father: "Father, into
thy hands I commend my spirit. . . . Father, forgive them,
they know not what they are doing . . . It is achieved."

Since Christ was God, in his humanity assumed by the
Person of the Word, could it be otherwise?

The Resurrection of Jesus

It was the miraculous fact of the resurrection which
chiefly antagonized the Jews against the Christian faith.
They regarded it as merely a trick of the apostles. After
convicting them of their sin by the story of the Passion and
crucifixion, pseudo-Peter sets out to convince them of the
truth of the resurrection.

He does not consider the inspired Gospel sufficiently
convincing. The chief objection of the sceptics ran thus:
who actually saw Christ come forth from the tomb? When
the sacred Text was opened the answer could soon be
given: no one, neither the Roman guard, nor the holy
women, nor the apostles, still less the Jews.

According to the Gospel the soldiers placed on guard at
the tomb only saw the angel who announced the resurrection:

> And suddenly there was a great trembling of the earth,
> because an angel of the Lord came to the place, descending
> from heaven, and rolled away the stone and sat over it . . .
> so that the guards trembled for fear of him, and were like
> dead men [And the holy women who had come to visit the
> tomb, and found themselves at this instant in the soldiers'
> company, saw nothing more. The angel simply told them of
> the miracle which had happened:] I know well that you
> have come to seek Jesus of Nazareth, the man who was
> crucified. He is not here; he has risen as he told you. Come
> and see the place where the Lord was buried. You must go
> in haste, and tell his disciples that he has risen from the

dead; and now he is going on before you into Galilee.
(Matt. 28. 2-4, 5-7.)

It is quite true that none of his associates, either men
or women, saw Christ come forth from the tomb. The
evangelists have given as substantial evidence, the empty
tomb, the shroud and the linen clothes. These proofs were
regarded as inadequate. It was maintained that the body
of Jesus had been taken away, for it had not been guarded
during the first night. It was only in the Saturday morning
that:

> The chief priests and the Pharisees gathered in Pilate's
> presence, and said, Sir, we have recalled it to memory that
> this deceiver, while he yet lived, said, I am to rise again
> after three days. Give orders, then, that his tomb shall be
> securely guarded until the third day; or perhaps his dis-
> ciples will come and steal him away. If they then say to the
> people, He has risen from the dead, this last deceit will be
> more dangerous than the old. (Matt. 27. 62-4.)

There remain the apparitions. But they too have provoked scepticism among Christ's detractors. Jesus first
appeared to simple women, prone to visions, whose witness was not even accepted by the apostles themselves:
"But to their minds the story seemed madness, and they
could not believe it" (Luke 24. 11).

And when, in their turn, the disciples relate the different
manifestations of the risen Lord, is it possible to take at
all seriously the witness of those only too interested in
maintaining the fraud?

It was to circumvent these difficulties, which he doubtless thought insurmountable that pseudo-Peter invented a
complete account which was extremely plausible. His first
care was to describe even the very coming forth from the
tomb by surrounding it with a host of eyewitnesses and
the support of unimpeachable guarantees.

On the very evening of Good Friday, without waiting,

the scribes and Pharisees, so we are told, demand of Pilate
the body of the dead man. The burial was carried out, not
merely by the care of Joseph of Arimathea, the friend of
Jesus (Matt. 27. 57-60, and parallel passages), but also
by the crowds of his enemies. With the Roman guard, the
chiefs of the Jews "rolled a great stone, then all those who
were there combined to push it against the entrance of the
tomb" (verse 32).

As if these precautions were not enough, the Jewish
authorities shared the sentry duty with the Roman cen-
turion and his men, not without first of all placing no less
than seven seals on the tomb. The result was, that, "early
in the morning of the Sabbath a crowd came out from
Jerusalem and the surrounding district to inspect the sealed
tomb" (verse 34).

All suspicion of fraud is thus removed: there could be no
fear that the Apostles would carry the body away. But as
a crowning guarantee pseudo-Peter makes the Jewish
elders together with the Roman soldiers witness the actual
rising of Christ. The mystery is made visible for them. It
was the Roman guard who were present, without any panic,
at the preliminaries of the resurrection, the coming of
the two angels heralding it:

> There was a great noise in the heaven. They saw the
> heaven open and two men, all resplendent, come down and
> go up to the tomb. The stone which had been set against the
> door rolled away of its own accord to one side. . . . When
> they saw this the soldiers woke up the centurion and the
> elders who were there on guard also. (Verses 36-8.)

This alarm allowed the Jewish elders and the pagan
soldiery to collect together unexpectedly to witness the
coming forth from the tomb. At this moment the two angels
who had come down from heaven went into the tomb, and
after a moment brought Christ out, returning from death
to life. This is the strange phenomenon:

They [all those watching] saw three men coming out of the tomb: two angels bearing the other [Christ] and a cross which followed them. The head of the two first touched the sky, but the head of the one they were carrying penetrated into the sky. And they [the witnesses] heard a voice from heaven saying, Have you preached to the dead? And the cross was heard to answer, Yes. (Verses 39-42.)

A strange vision, in which Christ, without being named, but followed by the cross, came up from the abode of the dead, supported by angels. Probably his unlimited height stands for his divinity, which surpasses the angels, heavenly giants. There is nothing real in the picture: it is all symbolical of a mystery. The author has added no historical evidence of the resurrection, which was not seen but definitely attested by the evangelists. Need we emphasize that the gaps in the Gospel story are not sufficient to disprove the reality of the event. Pseudo-Peter is quite wrong in minimizing the formidable evidences provided by Scripture. For if the miracle of the resurrection must remain for all time a supreme mystery, the witness of the apostles has offered to sane criticism indisputable proofs of authenticity. The empty tomb and the various apparitions of the risen Christ speak for themselves; on the other hand, the Jews certainly would not have had to bribe the Roman soldiers (Matt. 28. 13) if these had not been compulsory witnesses of the miraculous opening of the tomb. As for the apostles, at the outset they would hardly have doubted the women's story if they had concerted together to put about the story of Jesus' survival. These good men were neither deceived nor fanatics. It is the living Christ—of flesh and bone—who compelled conviction after all the anxieties and uncertainties which followed his death. And what ulterior motive could they have had in any fraud? The resurrection involved their lives in exacting spiritual and moral requirements which were to lead them to the witness of blood, to martyrdom itself. Humanly speaking they had nothing to gain.

If the gospel of Peter is, then, without any historical value, are we to reject it outright? No. Scholars are agreed that not only is there no trace of doctrinal error in it, but that it is interesting evidence of a first attempt at a Christian theology at the beginning of the second century. What specially characterizes it, apart from its unfortunate anti-Jewish polemic, is its eagerness to defend the divinity of Christ. The resurrection scene is illuminating on this point. Leaving aside historical accuracy, the author enters the realm of apocalyptic visions. The imagery which he uses is the symbolism such as we find frequently in Jewish or Christian "revelations": the heavens opened, from which loud sounds come forth, the huge stature of Christ and the angels, the appearance of the cross, all highly Semitic expressions meant to indicate the mystery of the resurrection in which God intervenes as sovereign and Christ proves his divinity.

This theology is certainly very defective in form, but the Christians who had been Jews knew that its images were not to be taken literally. We of the West must not, then, judge this narrative on strictly historical lines. It is, under conventional literary forms, a theological treatise which sets out to proclaim our faith in Christ who by his divinity has come forth from death as a conqueror.

THE GOSPEL OF NICODEMUS

When the Christian recites the Creed, after acknowledging that the Lord Jesus "was crucified, dead and was buried," he immediately adds that "He descended into hell."

We have here an article of faith which does not fail to seem mysterious despite its straightforward announcement. Why is this descent into hell put between Christ's burial and resurrection? The Gospel account makes no mention of it. Yet the question cannot be evaded—what became of our Saviour while he lay in death? It is not enough to reply that he lay in the earth: if his body was dead his soul was indissolubly united to the divine Word, and did not cease to be truly living, for this was a necessary consequence of the Person of the Word being incarnate in Christ. During the time of his death, our Saviour then was not inactive. The Epistle of St Peter twice indicates his mysterious activity: "And it was in his spirit that he went and preached to the spirits who lay in prison" (1 Peter 3. 19). "That is why dead men, too, had the gospel message brought to them" (1 Peter 4. 6).

To us this language must appear obscure, but not for those who are familiar with the Bible. It was in Shcol, the underworld place of waiting for the dead, that those who during life hoped for the Messiah awaited their deliverance. There was no salvation for them until Christ should come and conquer the powers of darkness and rescue the souls of the just from the unfortunate consequences of original sin. It was through his death that Jesus conquered the Devil and his work, sin. This victory opened the gate of salvation to the souls of the old Covenant. The risen Saviour could say to St John in the Apocalypse: "Do not be afraid; I am before all, I am at the end of all, and I live. I, who underwent death am alive, as thou seest, to endless ages, and I hold the keys of death and hell" (Apoc. 1. 17-8).

The Descent to Hell

It is the profound truth of Christ holding "the key of death" and of hell that the gospel of Nicodemus strove to depict in a vision of apocalyptic colours. The work only dates back to the fourth century, and is therefore relatively late, but it has a certain archaic flavour.

The scene is set on the day after the resurrection. Two dead men who have come back to life at the very moment when Jesus rose[1] are asked by the Jews to write their experience of beyond the grave to reveal to them the mystery of the "secret works" of Christ during his descent into hell. This these men do and this is their story. When they were wandering with the dead "in the depths of thick darkness" a great light suddenly enveloped them. Was it not the cloud of salvation? The sleeping nether world shook off its drowsiness. All the just, from Adam, "the Father of the human family," down to those who had just died, rise up. The patriarchs and prophets announce that their prophecies are to be fulfilled. John the Baptist, who had only lately come there, proclaims: "I have come to announce that shortly the Son of God himself, a star from on high, will visit you."

The two witnesses describe the terrors of Hell when confronted with the exultation of the righteous. Satan and his minions are dismayed. The man whom they thought they had destroyed has eluded their grasp. While they are questioning one another, they hear this shout: "Swing back, doors, higher yet, higher, immemorial gates, to let the King enter in triumph."

Then Hell realizes that it has been deceived, and with astounding volte-face, sets upon its own prince, Satan, now considered incompetent. The perfunctory struggle which ensues is a matter of no surprise. Hell is disarmed. The saints rejoice and David hurls back at the devils:

> Did I not foretell to you when I was yet alive? . . . the Lord has broken the brass gates and shattered the bars of iron asunder. . . . He is the Lord of Armies . . . he looks down from heaven to hear the groans of the captives and to deliver the children of death. And now foul and loathsome

[1] See Matt. 27. 52-3.

Hell, open your gates, that the King of Armies may enter in.[2] [At the mention of the Messianic prophecies:] while David was yet speaking, the Lord of Glory in human flesh entered into hell. He lightened the eternal darkness, broke the indissoluble bonds (of death) and visited us with his victorious strength. [Then Hell admitted its defeat:] You have cast death aside in the tomb and come among us living. See, you are free in the midst of death and bring confusion to our legions. Who are you, then, who have delivered those held captive by original sin and have restored to them their first state? [Jesus reveals his Omnipotence in asserting his dominion over Satan, and says to Hell:]

Satan, your head, will be bound to you for all eternity instead of my righteous ones, Adam and his children. (Gospel of Nicodemus, 5-7.)

When the devil has been chained, Jesus releases the faithful ones: "Come to me, all my children, who have been made in my image and likeness." Immediately the company of the elect assembles round the Saviour, beseeching him to place the sign of the cross over these regions of Hell, as the sign of his victory. Having done so, Jesus then "took Adam by the right hand and he went up out of hell, with all the saints following him."

The ascent from the nether world is completed in heaven, whither Christ, by his glorious ascension, led the redeemed. The two narrators cannot describe this final episode of the liberation of their brethren from the tomb because they themselves have been favoured with a continuation of life here on earth.

This vision of the kingdom of shadows is perfectly orthodox, despite its imaginary character. It is a popular presentation of the Christian faith in Christ's descent into hell. This faith is based on the fact that Christ died to re-

[2] The allusion here is to Psalm 23.

deem all men from their sin; owing to the fall of the first man their solidarity in his sin had included all succeeding generations. If Jesus came forth from the tomb victorious and overcame sin by his innocent death and freed mankind from the powers of evil, then it was fitting that the first to benefit should be the souls of those just ones who had lived in the hope of redemption. The liberation of the saints of the Old Testament is, then, only a natural consequence of the paschal mystery, of which St Paul speaks, when in writing to the Ephesians, he tells them that Jesus, before ascending to heaven, "had gone down, first, to the lower regions of the earth."

And what was the reason for this visit to the underworld? "So that everything in heaven and on earth and under the earth must bend the knee before the name of Jesus, and every tongue must confess Jesus Christ as the Lord, dwelling in the glory of God the Father" (Phil. 2. 10). This explains why, in the gospel of Peter also, the voice of the Heavenly Father is heard asking the Son at his resurrection, "have you preached to the dead?"

When he proclaimed the Good News of Salvation to the kingdom of the dead, Christ delivered the souls which until then had been under the power of the Devil and of death. He subjected all creation to his dominion. We may conclude with these words of St Paul: "That was why Christ died and lived again; he would be Lord both of the dead and of the living" (Rom. 14. 9).

CHAPTER XV

THE LEGEND OF THE
APOSTLES

The New Testament has extremely little to say on the later career of the apostles. The Acts of the Apostles, of course, follows the course of St Paul's missionary journeys, but it stops just as we expect to read of his death. And of Peter, an almost obtrusive figure at the beginning, the book abruptly loses all trace. It is only through his Apocalypse that we have any hint that John lived to extreme old age. As for James and Andrew, apart from the Gospel we know nothing more than their names. Where were they sent to bear witness to the risen Christ? Where, and how, did they die? Scripture tells us nothing.

Very early, it is true, traditions of unequal value and origin were current on their lives. So do we learn of the martyrdom of Peter and Paul at Rome, and the long residence of John in Asia. The early Christians were eager to know more about each of these witnesses of Jesus. It was inevitable that there should come into being whole histories covering all the activities and heroic end of the apostles, embroideries to a great extent on the scraps handed down by Tradition.

Thus towards the end of the fourth century we find united in a single corpus the apocryphal acts of Peter, Paul, John, Andrew and Thomas. These works, though of different dates and by different authors, are more or less orthodox, but they afford valuable information on the Christian ideals pervading the communities from which they came in the second and third centuries.

THE ACTS OF PETER

The apostolic activities of the Prince of the Apostles is chiefly known to us through a Latin work, the Vercelli Acts, which is a mid-third century recasting of a Greek original, now lost, which may date back to 200-210.

We read there of the strife at Rome between Peter and Simon the Magician. This latter, who was one of the founders of Gnosticism in Palestine (Acts 8. 9-24) had come to corrupt the Christians of Italy.[1] Peter, coming quickly on the scene, completely vanquished the impostor in the presence of a great crowd. But Peter's own miracles now begin to have the appearance of magic: a dog acquires a human voice, a fish is restored to life, and after other unlikely manifestations, Simon, when flying through the air, is brought down at the prayer of Peter.

At the sight of these marvels, the Christian community, which had wavered, is restored to its first fervour. But the Prefect of Rome then seeks to put to death this too powerful witness of Christ. It is here that the narrative of Peter's martyrdom begins. His friends urge him to flee and hide: "But as he passed through the city gate, he saw the Saviour coming into Rome. He asked him, Lord, where are you going. And the Lord answered, I am going to Rome to be crucified" (Acts of Peter, 25).

Peter then understood that he must die like Jesus. He returned to the city and was soon arrested and condemned

---

[1] We know that he practised magic, calling himself the possessor of that "Power of God" which is called "the Great": one of the cosmic divinities of Gnosticism.

to be crucified. Joyfully, he gave himself to the executioners that he might continue the passion of Christ in his own body. He asked and was granted to "be crucified head downward to repair the fall of Adam who turned the world upside down" (ibid.).

The work is by a Catholic, free from dogmatic error. It is a species of fiction, dealing freely with facts, which celebrated the arrival and then the glorious death of Peter at Rome: facts established by tradition and recognized by modern criticism.

THE ACTS OF PAUL

This work has come down to us in three fragments which primitively were joined together. The most interesting are the Coptic version called "The Acts of Paul and of Thecla" and the "Martyrdom of Paul."

In these narratives (of which a Greek fragment of the fourth century was found by Schmidt at Fayum in Middle Egypt in 1934) the Apostle is seen in his rôle of the intrepid missionary in Asia and in Greece. His teaching, however, is mostly concerned with continence, which seems to sum up, for him, all holiness. He is accused of forbidding young people to marry. The fact is that on all sides he inspired vocations to the celibate life: such is the case of Thecla, a young female convert who refused marriage and died a martyr to preserve her virginity. It is not long before Paul soon has to suffer for his teaching. After many vicissitudes he is taken prisoner at Rome under Nero and condemned to death by beheading. But his death lacks reality; milk flows from his body instead of blood, and the martyr is scarcely dead before he shows himself to his enemies in repeated apparitions.

The work has scarcely any historical value, though it informs us on the ascetical ideals prevalent during the second century in certain Christian circles. The author was a Catholic: according to Tertullian he was an "Asian priest," who undoubtedly wrote before 180. He set out to contest the Gnostic ideas of carnal licence, but his over-violent reaction led him perilously close to Encratism: according to him, for Paul chastity is the whole of Christian perfection; in addition, instead of a Gospel counsel it becomes an absolute obligation for salvation. Because of its lofty moral tone the Fathers had at first a high opinion of the *Acta Pauli*. But on account of the discreditable use made of them in the fourth century by the Manicheans, St Jerome and his successors condemned this apocryphal writing.

THE ACTS OF JOHN

It is difficult to establish these acts in their primitive text, as we do not possess more than a third of them, in comparatively late fragments. There are two Greek manuscripts and a Latin translation. These texts, in accordance with more authentic Tradition, speak of John's long sojourn in the province of Asia. But the preaching attributed to him is heretical. Several features of Jesus' early life are tainted with the Docetist[2] heresy. "Sometimes," says John, "when I wished to put my hand on him, I found that his body was material and substantial; at other times, when I touched him, he was immaterial and without a body, as if he did not exist" (Act. XCIII).

Sometimes the apostle puts Gnostic language into Christ's mouth. Thus, after the resurrection, the Saviour appears to John under the form of a bright cross, and says to him:

[2] The heresy which considered that Christ had only an apparent human body.

This cross of light is called by me sometimes word, sometimes mind, sometimes Jesus, sometimes Christ, sometimes door, . . . sometimes bread, sometimes seed . . . sometimes Father, sometimes Spirit. . . . Yet, in truth, as conceived of in itself and as spoken of to you, it is . . . the power which conserves all things unstable.

Apart from these ramblings, due to Gnostic tendencies, the story of the end of John's life has Encratite leanings. St John who, despite what St Mark seems to imply (Mark 10. 38-9), did not die a martyr, feels in extreme old age his end approaching. Before having his grave dug and lying in it to sleep in the Lord, he utters certain words on his virginity which imply a contempt for marriage.

On the whole the Acts of John reveal a Catholicism contaminated by the prevalent errors—Gnosticism, Docetism and Encratism. It is a compilation issuing from the Johannine milieu of Asia, the original of which may date from the middle of the second century.

THE MARTYRDOM OF ANDREW

The Acts of Andrew have only come down to us in fragments. The most interesting are those found in Gregory of Tours in the fourth century, called "The Book of the Miracles of the Blessed Apostle Andrew." But apart from this collection of very unlikely marvels, we have several independent narratives of Andrew's martyrdom. The oldest, in the form of a letter, in Latin, is attributed to the "priests and deacons of Achaia."

It is stated in this that Andrew wished to convert the proconsul of the town of Patras, and explained to him the mystery of the cross. The cruel pagan, in order to test Andrew's teaching, ordered him to undergo the most savage crucifixion. Andrew was to be fixed to a cross in the form of X, so that his body might be burst asunder. But Andrew went to his fate singing a hymn to the Cross of such sweetness that the liturgy has adopted it for his feast (November 30th): "Hail, cross consecrated by the body of Christ and adorned as with pearls by his members . . . O good cross . . . long desired . . . faithfully loved . . . take me from among men and give me to my Master, so that he who redeemed by your aid, may through you take me to himself."

CHAPTER XVI

REVELATIONS ON THE

AFTER LIFE

The Epistles of St Paul and the Apocalypse of St John drew the attention of the first Christians principally to man's final destiny and the after life. But Scripture was far from satisfying men's thirst by these revelations about the future. Men were curious to know how and when the end of the world would occur, and especially of the nature of the life in store for the saved and the damned in Paradise and in Hell, seeing that Scripture was so reticent in these matters. Inspired by imagination, there flourished the apocryphal epistles and apocalypses which sought to "reveal" the secrets of the after life.

THE EPISTLE OF THE TWELVE APOSTLES

This was unknown until our own time when it was discovered by M. Schmidt in 1895. It is a Catholic work in Coptic, in the form of an encyclical letter from Jerusalem to all the Churches to communicate the revelations which Jesus after the resurrection, is alleged to have confided secretly to the twelve apostles. We find the signs which are to herald the end of the world set down with astonishing certainty, and that the return of the Lord is expected before the year 150 and so on. This last detail dates this letter from the beginning of the second century. Issuing from a Jewish-Christian milieu, it is orthodox, but betrays an esoteric aspect which likens it to the apocalypses of which we are going to speak.

THE APOCALYPSE OF PETER

"Apocalypse" means Revelation. St John in his Apocalypse had only partly drawn aside the veil which hides the heavenly realities from human eyes. Pseudo-Peter in his "revelation" discloses these secrets in full measure. The work which was cited in the second century, became lost, but has been restored by two modern discoveries. In 1886 Bouriant unearthed a fragment of it in Greek in the tomb of Akhmin where he had also unearthed the gospel of Peter. Then a complete version in Ethiopian was discovered, totally forgotten, in a library at Oxford.

The apocalypse of Peter purports to be a secret revelation of Jesus to him. The primary object is a long and detailed description of Hell. The inspired Gospel had simply used imagery to describe the pains in store for the damned: these were particularly "the gehenna" [1] of fire (Matt. 5. 22); "the fiery lake that burns with brimstone" (Apoc. 19. 20); "the darkness without, where there will be weeping and gnashing of teeth" (Matt. 8. 12); "the worm which eats them there never dies" (Mark 9. 47). What scope for excitable imaginations! Pseudo-Peter has conjured up the singular picture of the different kinds of penalties being reserved for different categories of sinners: the unjust, murderers, the impure, etc. Here is an instance:

> There is an enormous pit; in this are all those who have acted unjustly. The tormenting angels will be on the watch

[1] The name of a ravine near Jerusalem where the Jews had burnt victims to the god of fire, Moloch.

. . . and will make them burn in the tormenting fire . . .
Murderers and their companions will be thrown in the fire
at the place filled with wild beasts, the worms which gnaw
them will be as numerous as the clouds of darkness. . . .
Near this fire is another pit, very large and very deep . . .
in this women who have caused the untimely birth of their
children and hindered the Lord's work will be cast in up to
their neck. . . .

This passage is very ancient and has its interest, for it
is the first Christian attempt to picture Hell. And we know
what influence this picture has had on the mind of Christians right up to our own day. Hell as shown under these
terrifying exterior forms and by over-materialized pains
has too often caused it to be forgotten that it is less a place
than a state of utter loss of God and his love.

THE APOCALYPSE OF PAUL

The apocalypse of Paul, which is later than that of Peter,
must have been compiled in the middle of the third century. The copies we have of it, in Greek (fourth century)
and in Latin (fifth century) shows us how these earlier
ideas on the after life have been developed.

The starting point of this "revelation" seems to be the
vision which Paul declared he could not describe in human
terms: "There is a man I know who was carried out of
himself in Christ, fourteen years since . . . this man, at
least, was carried up into the third heaven. I can only tell
you that this man . . . was carried up into Paradise, and
heard mysteries which man is not allowed to utter" (2 Cor.
12. 2-4).

But what the Apostle hesitated to reveal is brought by
the Apocalypse into broad daylight. First, the pseudo-Paul
has received valuable light on the rôle of certain angels
who are the "guardians" of each man and woman and

who: "come to adore God and to offer to him the good and bad works done by each."

Then the visionary is present at the particular judgement of a soul just released from this earth by death, and ready to receive the first award of his deeds. Lastly and supremely, the writer is conducted by an angel through the intricate ways of the heavens, and allowed to visit both Heaven and Hell. In Paradise he is shown the "promised land," prepared above for those who live in hope for it. Mysterious things are awaiting them there, as for instance, a white lake, the colour of milk, in which those converted at the last hour are baptized before entering the "city of Christ." In this latter there are the four rivers of the garden of Eden (Gen. 2. 11-14). The first, of honey, nourishes the prophets; the second, of milk, the innocent; the third, of wine, quenches the thirst of the patriarchs; lastly a river of oil gladdens the joyful, "those who have given themselves to God with all their heart and are humble."

In the heart of the city, so rich in all good things, are set thrones surrounding a central altar. Those who were the most humble are seated on these thrones, whose ignorance makes it to be said of them that they have the faith of a child. They are where they are through their uprightness of intention and obedience to the divine will. Close to the altar, as if to receive the praises of these categories of the elect, stands David. He sings the Alleluia of eternal happiness, accompanying himself on the harp, to which all the saints give answer.

The angel leads the Apostle from Paradise to Hell. The contrast is abrupt. Instead of the region of happiness and joy he finds suffering and gloom. It is first a deceptive vision of an immense river of fire and unfathomable gulfs. A different torment is appropriated to each category of the damned. The tepid are cast into the river of fire, those, that is, who were neither good nor bad; a priest and a bishop find themselves there with careless layfolk. In the unfathomable gulfs the usurers are struggling, eaten by worms; also the mad, forced to eat their tongues; magicians, plunged into blood up to their lips; adulterers and fornicators, their hands manacled in red-hot chains. Then, in a place covered with snow and ice, the unjust and merciless are perishing from the cold, naked and barefoot. This nightmare vision moves Paul to bitter tears of distress. The angel also weeps while cries of misery and pleas for mercy come up from the company of the damned. At the Apostle's prayer, the Archangel Michael allows them a slight alleviation of their sufferings. Then the Apostle returns to Paradise where he meets the Virgin Mary, who congratulates him on being the means of leading so many souls to their eternal rest.

This great picture—at once so intriguing and so terrifying—has inspired a host of medieval legends and numerous artistic works. And as the reader will recognize, it found its supreme expression in Dante's *Divina Comedia*.

All these apocryphal letters and apocalypses have in common this attempt to pass themselves off as secret revelations made by Jesus to a chosen group, either the apostolic college or a particular apostle. But all this secrecy has absolutely no place in the New Testament. Christ's teaching on the end of the world and what he says of the life to come are part of his public teaching, addressed to all. Of course, certain visions of St Paul or of St John might allow us to believe in private revelations of the Master. But, then, if these revelations have not been made public, it is precisely because they do not concern the universal message of salvation.

The above works, then, are the product of a certain Christian Gnosticism born among the Judaizers. They did not fail to inspire the real Gnostics to fabricate their own ultra secret and fatuous revelations. Yet, the first speculations on the final destiny of man, in spite of their fantastic details, by reason of their fundamental orthodoxy, are a primitive witness to the Catholic faith in the realities of Heaven and Hell.

THE ULTIMATE VALUE

OF THE APOCRYPHA

We have now pursued our study of this varied literature which grew up in the early days of Christianity. We can now give a brief chronological summary. In the first century there are in the Jewish Christian milieu the gospels to the Ebionites and Nazarenes. The second century shows the beginning of an unusual and prolific literary output. It is then that we have the gospel of James on Mary, and that of Peter and Nicodemus on the Passion, which came from the Church, while the Gnostics produced their secret gospels according to Philip, Thomas, Matthias or others.

This flood of apocryphal writings was not confined to "gospels." Continuously from the second to the fourth century there is a series of different works; particularly, the acts of various apostles, Peter, John and Paul. There are also the epistles, that of the twelve Apostles, and then the apocalypses attributed to Peter and to Paul.

At the same time the earlier works are still in circulation, edited and recast. After the book of the passing of Mary, there is the gospel of the pseudo-Matthew and then the Arabian and Armenian gospels of the Infancy appear in the field. In addition must be mentioned those very miscellaneous and superficially Christian works which were in circulation in these earliest times.

What was the attitude of the Church when she was confronted with this motley crowd of writings, claiming her authority in the person of the apostles themselves? At once firm and yet flexible, showing her wisdom and prudence. And it is this that is shown us by the historical rejection of these apocryphal writings and the judgement of their worth given by ecclesiastical authority.

THE REJECTION
OF THE APOCRYPHAL WRITINGS

It would be quite wrong to imagine that the infant Church, as a tribunal, was able to decide definitively and immediately about the traditions which arose, within and without her fold. We must not forget that in the second century the successors of the apostles and the communities in their care were still linked to the living voice of Christ and his apostles by the chain of oral Tradition. Every care was then taken in collecting what was fixed in writing from this still living source.

On the other hand, and it is a remarkable fact, by the end of the first century it was generally known throughout the Roman Empire that the essential element of Jesus' message was contained in the four Gospels of Matthew, Mark, Luke and John.

Towards 150 this certainty was expressed with unequalled vigour in the work of St Irenaeus, the champion of the authentic tradition of the Gospel against the false teaching of the Gnostics. In the middle of the second century Irenaeus proclaimed in no uncertain terms that there is only one Gospel "in four forms" (the four books mentioned) to which nothing can be added, nothing taken. And he concludes: "Those who would destroy the essence of the Gospel are mad and insensate and extremely daring, as also those who would increase or diminish the number of its forms: the former for thinking they have found a more profound truth, the others for destroying the work of God" (*Adversus Haereses,* 3, 11, 8).

It is certain, then, that very early the Church, menaced by incipient heresies within and without drew up an inventory of her faith. She clearly recognized the true Testament of Jesus in what St Justin calls "the memories of the Apostles" handed on by the authorized witnesses of his actions and his words.

This certainty is also based on the very life of the Christian communities. This same St Justin tells us that during the celebration of the Lord's Supper the four Gospels were publicly read:

On what is called the day of the Sun there is a meeting of all who live in cities or the country; and the memoirs of the apostles or the writings of the prophets are read as long as time allows" (*Apology.* I. 65).

This is convincing evidence that our Gospels were received as the Word of God in the same way as the books of the Old Testament. Thus it was not only the Gospel texts which were counted as inspired Scripture in the Church. The Epistles of St Paul, collected into a single corpus by the end of the first century, also enjoyed the same distinction.

But it was essential to make an increasingly careful distinction between the assortment of works claiming to be by an apostle. Lists were therefore drawn up of the books which could be accepted as authentic. What criterion governed this choice?

Tertullian, a lawyer, answers this question with astonishing legal precision: "We maintain in the first place that the title 'Gospel' has the apostles for guarantee, since the Lord gave to them the charge of preaching the Gospel, and the companions of the apostles, not alone, but together with the apostles."

The Church, then, did not receive works if she could not be certain at least of their apostolic approbation, if not of their origin: the apostles and their successors with them were the "sureties" of authentic Tradition.

What is called the Canon of Scripture, that is, the official list of inspired books, was gradually compiled on this principle. The Greek word *kanon* means "rule," "measure," and it is used to designate the writings which the Church considered worthy to be considered as a norm and rule of faith for her children.

Admittedly the process was not achieved without some hesitation, which only proved the zeal for truth of the young Church. Lists which can be found among one or other of the Fathers from the first half of the second century remained incomplete. Some were too wide and included works which in due course were held as useful, but of a private character: as for instance the Epistle of Clement of Rome, and the Shepherd of Hermas. Others were too narrow, for they left out such inspired works as the Epistle to the Hebrews, or the Apocalypse of St John, and the catholic Epistles of James, Peter, and John. But this was an altogether passing feature.

It is very important to notice that the oldest list that we possess comes from Rome, and is called the Muratorian Canon from the name of the scholar (Muratori) who discovered it in Milan and published it in 1740. This is extremely valuable and gives us the list of sacred books which the Roman Church accepted at the end of the second century. In spite of gaps in the list we learn that together with the four Gospels are included—and nothing else—the majority of the books of the New Testament as we have it today.

Very early, then, and with amazing precision the Church authenticated her treasure, and defended it against all error. After the fourth century no doubt was any longer

possible about the books which were inspired by the Holy
Spirit for use in the Church: the Council of Carthage published the definitive list in 397. From that date there were
no other gospels, acts of apostles, letters or apocalypses
that could claim the approbation of the successors of the
apostles. In the sixth century, the decree, attributed to
Pope Gelasius, was published, which drew up a list of the
apocryphal books, that is, those rejected by the Church
from the canon of Scripture; in this we find listed the books
that we have discussed.

No one will argue that the Church had no right to make
this definitive choice. Most of the writings originated
within her fold, and she had received the Spirit of Truth
from her Founder (John 14. 26) so that she might assume
the charge of guarding and transmitting undefiled the
deposit of Faith. Jesus had said to Peter and the other
apostles with him (Matt. 16. 19): "All that you bind on
earth shall be bound in heaven . . ." (Matt. 18. 18).
This divine power of preserving the Truth was extended, it
need hardly be said, to the successors of the apostles, since
Jesus had said to the twelve: "And behold I am with you
all through the days that are coming, until the consumma-
tion of the world (Matt. 28. 20).

THE VALUE OF THE APOCRYPHAL WRITINGS

We have traced the historical rejection of the apocryphal
writings. We may now consider what value the Church
places on them. The reader is now in a better position to
understand why the apocryphal writings could not establish a claim to be included in the corpus of Scripture; from
every point of view the inspired Scripture is far superior to
its imitators. It grips us at once both by its literary beauty
and the great value of its subject matter because it introduces us straightway into the supernatural. The apocryphal

writings, on the contrary, even at their loftiest, never rise above the marvellous: we do not encounter in them the divine Mystery. The sobriety and restraint of the Gospel are the touchstone of its historical truth. Compared with it these narratives, devoid of all foundation, lack all probability. Renan himself saw them as the obverse of the Word of God, "the verbiage of an old gossip."

THEIR DOCTRINAL VALUE

But surely one of the reasons, and not the least important, for the rejection of the apocryphal writings has been their doctrinal weakness. We must here discriminate. Not all these writings have been rejected for doctrinal errors. From this point of view four categories of apocryphal writings can be distinguished. The first two comprise writings frankly heretical. There are first of all works openly contrary to the Christian faith, whose unorthodoxy is revealed by their very name: such for instance are the secret speculations of the Gnostics called "the sacred book of the Great Invisible Spirit" or the *Pistis Sophia*. In their regard there can be no hesitation. There are other Gnostic works, equally erroneous in content, which were concealed under the appearances of Christian teaching: it needed an Irenaeus and his like to refute the boasted apostolicity of these "gospels," attributed to Philip, Thomas and others.

The two final categories of apocryphal writings, on the other hand, are entirely different: these are writings which are indeed Catholic, but which are not sufficiently authenticated to be called apostolic in origin. We may mention the works which are Catholic in intention, but are not free from heretical tendencies, such as the gospels of the Judaizers which have a too Jewish sympathy; the acts of Peter and Paul, especially of John, marked, here and there, by Docetist or Encratic ideas. The first generation of

Christians utilized them before a particular community, broken off from the body of the Church, appropriated them for its own entirely heretical ends (such was the case with the gospel according to the Hebrews, used by the Nazarenes and the Ebionites; the acts of John used for their own purposes by the Manicheans). And then we have another category comprising works doctrinally irreproachable, which do not intentionally contradict the inspired Scriptures: these were the productions of popular Christianity, whose intentions were as excellent as they were badly expressed, and which had the intention of filling out the meagre data of the inspired Gospels. These would include the gospels of Mary, the stories of the Assumption, and of Christ's descent into Hell; the visions of the next world in the apocalypses of Peter and Paul.

The apocryphal writings were not, then, entirely bad, and it would be unjust to underestimate the importance and interest of these works for a better understanding of the early Church.

AS EXPRESSIONS OF ORAL TRADITION

Their first and greatest merit is to provide a clearer picture of the history of Christian origins. The religious excitement aroused in the ancient world by the proclamation of the Gospel would be largely unknown to us without this copious literature modelled on the Gospel stories.

Have we perhaps forgotten what an important part oral Tradition played in the production of the inspired books themselves? Increasingly, our canonical Gospels stand revealed as stages, essential stepping-stones, by the fixing in writing of that vast current of oral Tradition which preceded them, is in every way wider than them, and has not ceased with their appearance. With his disciples Christ behaved as a Jewish Rabbi, teaching by word of mouth.

All his actions and words went forth to the world by the voice of catechists, preachers and missionaries, before they were cast into definite narrative form. It would have been strange, in the circumstances, if the living voice of Tradition had not been altered here and there, even though preserving authentic elements of truth. The value of the apocryphal writings, as a marginal note to the Gospels, lies in this good grain which they have preserved.

We can now understand better why, though denying to them the authority of Scripture, and therefore (in the words of St Irenaeus) the rôle as "ground and pillar of our faith," the Church has made use of certain elements in the apocryphal writings. She has used as valuable witnesses of Tradition, on account of their great antiquity and doctrinal purity, the narratives of the life of Mary, Virgin and Mother, told by the Protevangelium and pseudo-Matthew. Without accepting the historical veracity which they claim, she recognizes in the narratives of the *transitus Mariae* a valuable expression of her faith in the Assumption of our Lady.[1] From the acts of Peter she has always held the tradition of the presence and martyrdom at Rome of Peter and Paul which modern scientific research has upheld. Finally, apocalyptic visions of Hell and Paradise have powerfully assisted Christians to understand the reality of divine judgement and of eternal life beyond the grave.

IN LITERATURE AND THE LITURGY

History has shown how, though the Church has been wise to set aside all non-inspired works from the public and official reading of the Word of God, she has not re-

---

[1] But the dogma is not based at all upon this form of the traditional "expression," but from a deeper theological understanding of the mystery of Mary in Scripture.

jected their use entirely. The Fathers held in high esteem all that came from living Tradition and we have seen how respect led them to accept the unwritten words of Jesus. Equally, the liturgy has not hesitated to borrow all that is best in the apocryphal writings to nourish the devotion of the faithful. A solid devotion to Mary finds there its source and strong support in contemplating the mysteries of the Mother of God: it cannot be denied that the charm and fervour of these narratives has strongly coloured Christian faith, especially in its more popular forms, in that golden age of legend, the Middle Ages. The cultus of the Blessed Virgin and of the saints which was so flourishing at that period obtained from these sources more than the element of the marvellous. The two most popular works in Europe between the twelfth and fifteenth centuries were the famous Golden Legend of James of Voragine and the Historical Mirror of Vincent of Beavais. These huge compilations of the lives of the saints reproduced almost entirely the apocryphal sayings of the gospel of the birth of Mary and the Acts of Pilate. Materials for representing to the people the "Mysteries" of our Lady and of the Passion were found in them.

Though these legends, which had assumed excessive importance, were rejected at the Reformation, Dante found in them—in the gospel of Nicodemus and the apocalypses of Peter and Paul—the inspiration of his journey to the abode of the dead and the living depicted in his *Divina Comedia*.

IN ART

If the reader still questions the influence of the apocryphal writings through the centuries, let him consider their influence on art. Is there a window, a capital in our great cathedrals, in which an observant eye will not notice, often interwoven with scenes from the Gospels many apocryphal details: the staff of Joseph which budded, when he wooed Mary; the ox and the ass at the crib; the visit of the Kings, etc.

The strangest and most intimate details in the life of Mary, or in the childhood of Jesus influenced the art of the Middle Ages and the Renaissance—the meeting of Joseph and Mary at the Golden Gate; the Annunciation at the fountain; the Dormition of our Lady. These are so many themes in celebrated pictures which often escape those not familiar with the apocryphal writings. In short, art, like literature and the liturgy, reveals to us the unsuspected place assumed by apocryphal literature in the mind and heart of Christian life down the ages.

This should be enough to show us that our judgement ought not to be more severe nor more indulgent than that of the Church, with her experience of more than a thousand years. It would certainly be an insult to the Scripture to put even the best of the apocryphal writings on the same level. If the Church does not accord to them the authority of the Word of God, we must not seek in them the source of our faith, as even in our own days, certain upholders of liberal criticism strive to do. But it would be equally unwise to undervalue the elements of historical and doctrinal truth which, not finding a place in the inspired books, have come down to us in these marginal writings, the products of a common Tradition.

SELECT BIBLIOGRAPHY

(An asterisk denotes works by non-Catholics)

In this series:

CRISTIANI, Léon: *Heresies and Heretics.*

DANIEL-ROPS: *What Is the Bible?*

STEINMANN, Jean: *Biblical Criticism.*

*BELL, H. I. and SKEAT, T. C.: *Fragments of an Unknown Gospel,* London, British Museum, 1935.

*CROSS, F. L. (Editor): *The Oxford Dictionary of the Christian,* London and New York, Oxford Univ. Press, 2nd edn, 1958.

*EVELYN WHITE, H. G.: *The Sayings of Jesus from Oxyrhyncus,* Cambridge and New York, Cambridge Univ. Press, 1920.

GRAYSTONE, G.: *The Dead Sea Scrolls and the Originality of Christ,* London and New York, Sheed and Ward, 1956.

GROLLENBERG, Luc. H., O.P.: *Atlas of the Bible,* London and New York, Nelson, 1957.

*JAMES, M. R.: *The Apocryphal New Testament* (Apocryphal Gospels, Acts, Epistles and Apocalypses), Oxford and New York, Oxford Univ. Press, corrected edn, 1953; *Latin Infancy Gospels,* Cambridge and New York, Cambridge Univ. Press, 1893.

LEBRETON, Jules, S.J.: *The Life and Teaching of Jesus Christ,* London, Burns Oates and New York, Macmillan, 1958.

LEBRETON, J., and ZEILLER, J.: *The History of the Primitive Church,* four volumes, London, Burns Oates and New York, Macmillan, 1942–8.

ORCHARD, B. (Editor): *A Catholic Commentary on Holy Scripture,* London and New York, Nelson, 1953.

*ROWLEY, H. H.: *The Dead Sea Scrolls and the New Testament,* London, S.P.C.K., 1957.

*SWETE, H. B.: *Gospel of Peter,* London, Macmillan, 1893.

*THERON, D. J.: *Evidence of Tradition,* Cambridge and New York, Cambridge, Univ. Press.

The Twentieth Century Encyclopedia of Catholicism

The number of each volume indicates its place in the over-all series and not the order of publication.

TWENTIETH CENTURY ENCYCLOPEDIA OF CATHOLICISM

All titles are subject to change.